TERRACOTTA TRAVELLERS

and other stories of life

Edited by
Claire Bell, James Cooper & Pete Court

TERRACOTTA TRAVELLERS AND OTHER STORIES OF LIFE
Series number: 8

Compilation copyright © Claire Bell, James Cooper and Pete Court 2023. Copyright of individual chapters remains with the author of those chapters.

All rights reserved. Other than for the purposes and subject to the conditions prescribed under the Copyright Act, no part of this publication may be reproduced, stored in a retrieval system, or transmitted in any form or by any means, electronic, mechanical, photocopying, recording or otherwise, without the prior permission of the publisher.

Cataloguing-in-Publication entry is available from the National Library of Australia http:/catalogue.nla.gov.au/.

This edition first published in Hackham, South Australia
November 2023
Published in Australia by Immortalise via Ingram Spark
www.immortalise.com.au

ISBN 978-0-6457721-2-8

Typesetting by Ben Morton
Front cover image is AI generated and AI repainted.
Cover layout by Ben Morton

Sponsors

We wish to thank the following organisations for their sponsorship of the Stories of Life creative writing competition and publishing venture:

Omega Writers
sponsoring the 2023 Stories of Life competition.

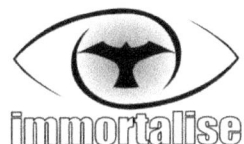

Immortalise
supporting the publication, sales and distribution of the 2023 anthology.

Tabor College of Higher Education
hosting the official launch of the 2023 anthology.

Introduction

Now in its eighth year, Stories of Life continues to encourage and equip people of faith to share their stories of God's grace and the love of Christ in their lives. With 42 original and compelling stories featured here, could this be our biggest issue ever? Quite possibly! What we know for sure is that more and more people each year are being moved to reflect on the many ways in which God is at work in their lives, and then sharing those stories with the wider world. And that's what Stories of Life is all about.

It's wonderful to see some familiar names among our list of contributing authors. Clearly, the power of storytelling is infectious, and we have some talented writers in our growing community. At the same time, it's encouraging to see so many new names – people who felt compelled to share their stories for the first time. To take up a pen in order to share a meaningful experience with an unknown reader is a leap of faith in itself, and we celebrate your courage.

Many of this year's contributors took advantage of our 'Feedback Month' during June, where writers are encouraged to send in drafts to receive feedback from our editors and previously published authors. By all reports, the process has proved most encouraging and rewarding, and exemplifies the gracious spirit of community building that Stories of Life is all about. Looking ahead to 2024, we'd encourage you to take advantage of this unique opportunity and also to encourage those in your own faith community or network of friends to do the same.

From ordinary encounters with the everyday to heart-wrenching life-and-death moments, the stories gathered here are truly diverse. While so much could be said of every story, they are perhaps best left to speak for themselves. That said, this year's title story (*Terracotta Travellers* – by Grant Lock) serves as a powerful example of what all the stories here do so well: taking a profound experience of God's presence in the world, and bringing it to life in a way that allows the reader to enter into that experience, to see and feel and question for themselves what the meaning of that encounter might be.

Like the 'terracotta travellers' on that bus, who witnessed an unexpected encounter shaped powerfully by the grace of God, every reader of every story here will be invited to wonder at what they have read. May these stories shake us out of our complacency, helping us to recognise the goodness and mercy of God in our own lives. May they prove a blessing to you as you read, and may they encourage you also to share your own story of life with those you know, and maybe even with those you don't!

James Cooper
For the 2023 Stories of Life Editing Team.

The Judges

Wendy Parker is an author, blogger and speaker. She is a member of the Australasian Christian Writers, Christian Writers Downunder, International Christian Fiction Writers, and Omega Writers. Currently studying a Bachelor of Theology with Alphacrucis College, Wendy's passion is to give people hope, and to see them reach their full potential by discovering their identity in Christ and the redemptive blood of Jesus. In her popular blog thebigvoiceonline.com and her podcast The Spacious Room, Wendy writes and speaks about the struggles of the everyday Christian life in her unique devotional style and draws from her experience of being part of church leadership for almost 20 years.

Wendy's debut non-fiction book, *Wounded And On The Run* was released by DOLL Ministries in October 2022 and she is in the process of writing her next book, *A Song Is Rising* which will be released towards the end of 2023. British by birth, but Aussie by choice, Wendy currently lives in Wollongong, Australia, and does life with her husband, Philip, their two grown children, and one spoilt chocolate Labrador named Rose.

Dr Mark Worthing is a Lutheran pastor, editor and prolific writer. His book *Martin Luther: A Wild Boar in the Lord's Vineyard* (Morning Star Publishing, 2017) was shortlisted for the 2018 Christian Book of the Year Award. His most recent works include *The Winter Fae, A Fantasy Novella* (Stone Table Books, 2018); and *Iscariot* (Morning Star, 2018), *The Sacred Life of Words: A Guide for Christian Writers* (Morning Start 2020), *Chelsea McAllister and the Bubblegum Effect* (Stone Table Books, 2021).

Contents

Introduction iv

The Judges vi

Rushing out the Door 1
    Leah Grant

Psalm 23 Isn't Just for Funerals 3
    Naomi Currie

Ask See Watch 10
    Rebekah Matson

Monster 13
    Juni Desireé Hoel

No More Tuna Mornay 15
    Liisa Grace-Baun

My Hand in His 21
    Simone Field

Musings at a Funeral 25
    Nesta Hatendi

Help from Heaven 31
    Hazel Barker

Piercing the Silence 34
    Jeanette Grant-Thomson

Uprooting 41
    Kathy Worthing

Mercy Mission to Ukraine 45
    Nadia Konik

Kisses for Me 51
    June Hopkins

Home Remedy 53
    DJ Blackmore

The Voice 59
    Karen Roper

Praying for Princess 61
    RJ Rodda

Dad and Jesse 65
   Jenny Woolsey

A Different Kind of Victory 72
   Nadia Konik

Solo with God 74
   Ruth C Hall

The Night Wanderer 80
   Wendy Zhong

Let the Children Come to Me 82
   Cherie Love

Learning to Ride a Bike 86
   Roslyn Bradshaw

A God-Given Glitch 89
   June Hopkins

Throw Your Heart Over the Fence 93
   Helena Stretton

Kindling 97
   Steph Penny

I Have Plans for You 104
   Alison Short

Baby in the Bathwater 106
   Morton Benning

The House that God Found 112
   Barry Horner

The Heart of a Midwife 116
   Esther Cremona

Dagger in the Heart 121
   Jo Wanmer

Classic Road Trip 123
   Roslyn Bradshaw

Fighting For Life 130
   Val Russell

God is Our Provider 135
   Cherie Love

Harbouring Beauty 137
  Catherine McAleer

The Pink Water Bottle 142
  Charles Yuen

Giving It All Up 146
  Hannah Lamb

Colours of Childhood 148
  Colleen Russell

Along for the Ride 153
  Ruth C Hall

Out of the Ashes 155
  Barbara McKay

Dear Friend 161
  Jo-Anne Berthelsen

Guitar Strums 163
  Diana Davison

People Matter 169
  Kylie Gardiner

Terracotta Travellers 171
  Grant Lock

Rushing out the Door
Leah Grant

'Put your shoes on,' then we hurry out the door. Small hands in mine, we walk through the carpark. There's a huddle of families signing in their children.

My husband and I find our seat and know we'll soon be dashing to get the boys home for lunch and naps.

As I sit and listen to church news, I set myself a goal. I will make the most of today. Instead of shying away at the dreaded 'meet-and-greet', I'm going to force myself out of my comfort zone and try to connect. Maybe I can put my insecurities aside to be a potential blessing.

There's a lady next to me who is likely over seventy and I'm unsure if she will be interested in talking to me in my thirties. But I make eye contact and introduce myself. My usual question at meet and greet time is, 'How long have you been coming to our church?' Which rarely leads the conversation anywhere. So I try something new. 'How was your week?' Simple, not rocket science. But I ask with genuine interest.

'Not great. The police arrived at my house late on Thursday, to tell me my husband had been found dead.'

I try to hide my wide eyes. That was, by far, the last thing I was expecting in reply. I shift in my seat and awkwardly enquire, 'I'm so sorry. What happened?'

The lady calmly describes her last interaction with her husband. He loved to fish and was heading out in the afternoon with all his gear on, big boots, and overalls. He slathered on his sunscreen and went to kiss her goodbye. She laughed and shooed him away, telling him, 'You are too greasy to kiss.' He teased her and held her hand. Then he placed a gentle kiss on the back of her hand, as though she was royalty.

He told her he'd be home by five and they could eat his catch for dinner. She was not filled with confidence and would have meat defrosted. Then he walked out the door.

The police told her his body was found in the shallow waves at the beach. It appeared he'd had a heart attack while wading, fishing on his own. Falling into the water, he then drowned.

I am deeply moved by the woman's vulnerability, sharing with a stranger her final and most intimate moment with her partner. I can see the sadness on her face and also love. Such love she had for him.

My mind is screaming, 'What do I say? This poor lady, how awful! I have no idea how to respond to this.' Awkwardly, I blurt out the obvious response, wishing I could think of something more comforting. 'I'm so sorry to hear that. You obviously loved him very much.'

I'm grateful that she shared her story with me. It's been six months since this meet-and-greet encounter and I'm still reminded of it often. Her story has encouraged me to hold my husband's hand a little tighter and to make the effort to kiss him as I rush out the door.

Psalm 23 Isn't Just for Funerals
Naomi Currie

Buzzzzz! Buzzzzz! Buzzzzz! My father and I bend over the opened beehive, clouds of bees swirling around us.

'Dad,' I say, 'Do you think – ow!' I slap a gloved hand at the spearing pain in my ankle.

Oh no, the cuff on the right leg of my heavy-duty bee suit has pushed up, exposing my ankle.

'Ow! Ow!' More stings in my right ankle. I scurry into some bushes, trying to brush the bees off so I can push the cuff back down without trapping bees underneath.

Suddenly my whole body burns with heat. I scratch at my ankle, then my stomach, then my face. My head throbs. My heart races. I touch my face; my lips feel enormous.

'Dad!' I shout, 'I'm reacting. Badly.'

Dad stares at me, a frame of honeycomb in his hands, and his gloves dark with bees. 'I didn't bring any antihistamines,' he says abruptly. 'Get away from the bees or you'll keep getting stung! Go back to the car!'

I squint at the car; it's a white blob on a strip of brown. Maybe sixty or seventy metres away, parked on the 4WD access track into the bushland where my hive is placed.

I start walking. The bee suit grows heavy. The pounding in my ears increases and the car starts to veer back and forth. It's growing dark. The sun must be setting.

Terracotta Travellers and other stories of life

Dad's voice. 'Get in the car! There are bees everywhere. We're a two-minute drive from home. Your sister has an EpiPen.'

Somehow, I'm in the car. Don't remember getting in. God, are you there? Lord, it's a bit scary. Lying down. Is it night? Is that why I feel so sleepy?

I can hear a dog, panting, rasping. Why is there a dog in the car? We don't own a dog.

Car moving. Car jerking. Bumpy. Reversing.

Dad's hand reaches out of the darkness and squeezes mine. 'Stay with me, girl, stay with me.'

That's the sort of thing they say in movies to people who are dying. No, I decide, I can't be dying. Last week the Lord spoke to me about writing for him. I can't write for him if I die now. Not logical.

'Thou art with me.' Is that a Bible verse? Can't remember where it is from.

Then nothing.

'Dad, the man on the phone wants to talk to you!' That's my sister's voice. But she wasn't there before. She was at home. The car's not moving. Am I swimming? Did I swallow lots of water? Is that why I can't breathe? Gotta cough it out. Too tired to cough.

Nothing again.

Is that my alarm clock? Is it time to wake up? No, it's an ambulance siren. Someone must be very unwell. Hope they are better soon.

Psalm 23 Isn't Just for Funerals

Car doors opening and slamming. Voices. Strangers' voices. Dad's voice. 'I've given her her sister's EpiPen.'

Not bees. Sheep. Something important I need to remember about sheep. That's it. 'The Lord is my shepherd,' I remember. Now I have nothing to worry about. I can sleep.

But there are voices still. 'Lovey, can you hear us? We're paramedics, we're here to help you, okay?'

'Mate, can we get this bee suit off her? How does it unzip? Never mind, where are the shears?'

Ripping sounds. Coldness. 'Can you hear us? Can you squeeze my hand?'

Did I squeeze it? I tried to.

Voices again. 'That's the second shot of adrenaline. Blood pressure 70 on…I can't get a reading. Nah, she's not responding properly. Turn it up, give her eight litres of oxygen.'

Nothing again.

Something about sheep and valleys. That's it. 'The Lord is my shepherd.' What's the rest of it? I should remember – they say it at funerals.

My body shudders. My legs jerk of their own accord, my arms strike out, hitting something or someone.

'Quick! She's convulsing! Lovey, just stay calm, okay, I need you to stay calm.'

She's the one sounding panicked. I am calm. I'm not dying. God said so. Maybe I should tell them that. But there's something on my face. A mask thing, I think.

My body shudders again. And again. Sheep. The Shepherd. 'Yea, though I walk through the valley of the shadow of death, I will fear no evil, for Thou art with me.' That's right. God is with me.

'Lovey, can you hear us, okay?'

'Yes.' My voice croaks the word out on the third attempt.

'Lovey, that's really good.' Her voice sounds suddenly brighter. 'Now, let's get you out of this car.'

Voices. A hard-edged thing touches my body. Some sort of rolling action, and then suddenly I'm level, flat. I'm rolling again, onto something softer, then being pushed. Car doors open, then there are clicking sounds and jolting.

'How are you going, Lovey? We'll take you to Flinders Hospital. Your mum's coming with you.'

Mum's here? Is my whole family here?

My body convulses again and again, but things hold me tight, hugging me close. Remember, the Lord is with me. The Lord is my Shepherd. Even in the valley. Going to be okay.

Car doors slam. Quiet. Just a few voices, Mum, and two ladies. One of the ladies is talking in a radio voice. The other lady is talking to me, asking me if I feel this or that. Have to be helpful and answer, even though my throat hurts. The ambulance starts moving. I hear a siren, a faint, far off siren. Jerky movements. Tut tut. My dad would shake his head at her. He always says I should drive smoothly. Turn gently. Accelerate smoothly. That's how you do it.

The ladies talk to each other. 'Give her another adrenaline shot,' Jerky Driver says, 'once I'm through this intersection.'

More jolting movements, then the vehicle slows.

'Okay, done.'

Didn't feel anything. But the darkness isn't so dark. It's getting greyer. The ambulance stops. Doors open, more clicking, more trundling. Corridors and machines and curtains and more people who ask too many questions and say too many names. Things slowly grow more distinct. A nurse fetches me heated blankets, a man who tells me he is a doctor waves a pair of tweezers at me and takes my shoe off. Did I put on clean socks this morning? He starts giggling, and I blush. That's right, I'm wearing my bee socks; bright blue socks with giant bees on them.

'You have nineteen puncture marks on your right ankle,' he says eventually. 'Nineteen stings. I saved your socks, but do you want any of your clothes as a souvenir? Or a piece of them?'

Nineteen stings. I look silently at the bundle of shredded clothes. I shake my head. The bee-suit, a jumper, my favourite t-shirt, leggings, tights. All I'm left with is underwear and a skirt. All those layers of protection, and yet undone by a faulty cuff.

The doctor leaves, and my mum appears. We sit and talk. Her eyes are red and everything she says is in an extra-bright tone of voice. She tells me it is noon. Less than an hour after I was stung.

The curtain is pushed aside for the umpteenth time, and a blonde woman appears in a green paramedic's costume. She asks how I am going, and steps closer, examining my face.

'I'm guessing you're one of the paramedics who helped me?' I say slowly, and try to smile. The skin feels so tight on my face, I must still look like a balloon. Must look a sight. I try to laugh off my self-consciousness. 'Thanks for saving my life.'

But she doesn't laugh. 'I've never seen an anaphylactic reaction that extreme,' she says quietly. 'We gave you five doses of adrenaline. You've also had a cocktail of steroids and antihistamines.'

So it hadn't just been a bizarre dream about bees and sheep?

The lady chats a little longer but leaves soon for another call.

'I was scared,' Mum says suddenly. 'For your life, and for all of us in the ambulance. That paramedic was the one driving. She was weaving all through traffic, and she went through a red light at a busy intersection. She was using the lights and siren, but she was going so fast, I was scared there would be an accident.'

'I just thought she was a jerky driver.'

The look on my Mum's face says everything.

'I…I don't think I comprehended my life was in danger,' I say slowly, 'except that I kept thinking about the Lord being my Shepherd and him looking after me.'

Mum swallows hard, her eyes wet. '"Yea, though I walk through the valley of the shadow of death, I will fear no evil, for Thou art with me." That's Psalm 23, verse four.'

I blink back tears. 'It's a very real promise of God's mercy and love. I learnt today that Psalm 23 isn't just for funerals.'

Ask See Watch
Rebekah Matson

'Wanna buy a watch?'

The tall, lanky boy called out as he was heading over to my car. I sat in the Piggly's Store carpark, home of 'Alice Springs' best ribs', waiting for my friend who was in the store. It was the best-known takeaway and small store in town, but not somewhere my friend or I had been in a long while. It was also known as an unsavoury part of town.

There was a group of boisterous teens at the back of the car park. Looking for mischief and jostling each other. They obviously had charged the boy now approaching the car to be the one to come and ask, and were now waiting, eyes peeled, on the interaction to see if they could get a part of the spoils.

As he got closer to the car, he repeated himself, 'Hey miss, you wanna buy a watch?'

I put my window up slightly and locked my door. I was unsure if his and his mates' motives were only to sell a watch, or if that was merely a distraction. He didn't appear scary, with his lopsided grin and big brown eyes, but Alice Springs was, sadly, known for opportune crime by bored youth, and so I was wary.

He arrived at my car door and said, 'Only twenty dollars.'

Less than an hour before, my friend who was in the store was telling me how a few weeks before, a young boy who would frequent our houses, often to get a cool drink or a feed, had this time come and stolen some money and a beautiful watch. A gift from her husband. She knew there was no way the money was coming back, and we followed up with the boy and told him we knew he had taken the watch and could he give it back. But he said someone else took it from him and he didn't know where it was. Seeing her distress at this loss, we had prayed together that God would help us locate it.

Now here I was, sitting out the front of a store I didn't usually frequent on the other side of town, and a stranger comes up to ask me if I want to buy a watch. I needed to see this watch!

'Can I see the watch?' I asked.

Any wariness I now had was overcome with curiosity, and I wound my window down. He stepped closer and pulled the watch from his pocket. There was no doubt about it. It was my friend's watch!

He asked again, 'You want it? Only $20.'

Very calmly, I replied, 'No, I'm not going to buy that watch. That is not your watch. That is my friend's watch and you're going to give it to me.'

He stared at me. I put my hand out of the window. He placed the watch in my hand. I quickly put my hand back in the car, clutching the watch in disbelief. All the time he was still staring at me like he was stuck and couldn't move.

I couldn't believe he had just handed me the watch!

He couldn't believe he had just handed me the watch.

My heart was racing. What was going to happen now? I looked around to see his friends running off without him.

He shook like he had just woken out of a trance and was about to run off, but I opened the door saying, 'You were sent here by God! We prayed, and he wanted you to bring that watch back to its owner. Well done!'

He was shocked and looked at me like I was crazy. He didn't know if he should run or what to do.

I told him I would like to shout him a cool drink and there was someone I would like him to meet. He followed me sheepishly into the shop, eyes darting, still not sure what I was going to do, or why he was still with me. I came into the shop and told my friend and handed her the watch and she hugged the boy. He was in shock. The brazen teenager now looking more like a wide-eyed little boy. The shopkeepers were watching on and wanted to know what was happening. I left out the part about him wanting to sell me the watch but told them that he had handed the watch back. We were so excited.

The boy got his lemonade and mumbled a thanks and ran off, perhaps concerned I might still call the police on him.

My friend and I left the store, buzzing and excited, and she rang her husband, almost shouting down the phone.

We knew that we had just witnessed a miracle. Every time I see her wearing that watch, we smile and shake our heads in awe.

Monster
Juni Desireé Hoel

Here I am. Sitting in church on a pew. Not listening to the preacher. Instead, I'm picturing myself getting up, walking to the door, throwing my head back and smashing it into the glass. The broken skin and dribbling blood matches how I feel on the inside. On the outside no-one sees.

After church, I'm sitting with some ladies drinking their cups of coffee around a table. One lady is sharing some problems she's going through, and I feel nothing. Instead of the expected empathy, I am empty. Blank. There's nothing in me left to care about someone else. Because every bit of me is doing everything it can to survive and smile here.

As I drive home, gripping the steering wheel with tears in my eyes, I listen to an interview on Vision Radio. A musician shares how she told a friend she felt so bad that she pictured driving her car into a pole. Her friend said, 'How about instead of expressing your feelings in a destructive way, you find a way to express them in a helpful way.' The musician started writing her feelings down as lyrics and that's how she came to compose songs.

By the time I'm home, I'm angry and sad and so full of pain and I don't know what to do with it all. I pace my room, digging my nails into my skin. I picture slamming my head into the plaster wall. All I want is someone to see this struggle. I pick up my Prismacolor pencils and sit on my bed with a pad of A3 cartridge paper. I use every colour in the box of 150 pencils. One frenzied hour of fury and anguish later and I can't look at the self-portrait I've drawn. It's too ugly. Too scary.

Shocked by my rage and loss of empathy, I meet with a psychologist. I tell her things I've never told anyone: the self-hatred, the self-harm. Like the musician's friend, she doesn't freak out. She doesn't think I'm crazy. She doesn't say I'm a bad person.

Sometime later, I pull out the self-portrait. It's still ugly. But it's not scary anymore. I stare at it and I feel seen. It is the most raw and real piece I've ever created. My monster. I thought I had to hide it. Hide my hurt. Hide my violent visions. Hide my struggle with self. Yet all along God saw my monster. He saw it at church, in the car, in my room. And he spoke to me through a musician, a psychologist, and a box of pencils, saying, 'You are seen. And I love you still.'

At my last session with the psychologist, I show her some of my drawings. They track the dark thoughts and feelings, and the tools and God that helped (and continue to help) me through them. I ask if she would like to keep one, if it might be useful in her work. She chose the monster.

No More Tuna Mornay
Liisa Grace-Baun

As I waved goodbye to my son, a strange feeling came over me. I could still see Tim's smile beaming back at me as I drove around the bend from his friend's place. My heart felt a little troubled, though I had no idea why. I prayed for Tim's safety and protection as I drove home.

Not long after arriving home, Tim's friend and his mother were knocking at my door. They were both frantically telling me that Tim had fallen from a tree and had hit the concrete head first from three metres high. I rushed out to the car where he was sleeping. Gently I picked him up and carried him inside concerned about the fragility of the nine-year-old body I held.

His face looked very pale as he vaguely responded to me waking him. I decided to carry him to his bedroom believing that it would do him good to sleep for awhile.

I returned to the kitchen, preparing tuna mornay, when suddenly I heard Tim screaming. It wasn't the kind of scream I'd ever heard before. I rushed to his room and found him cradling his head with his eyes closed, screaming, 'Let me die, let me die!'

Desperately, I tried talking to Tim, but he was non-responsive and seemingly unconscious. I hurried to the phone, called the hospital and was advised to bring him in immediately.

In a panicked state, I carried Tim into the car. I placed his infant sister Leah in her baby seat. Tim's older sister Krystle came along to help look after Leah. On arrival at the hospital, I put Tim in Leah's stroller and wheeled him in while Krystle carried Leah.

At the emergency triage window, the nurse checked Tim's pupils. In an urgent tone she called out to the orderly to quickly bring a bed. Within seconds Tim was being wheeled into a cubicle which was suddenly filled with doctors and nurses.

My heart was racing. Just one hour prior we were at home oblivious to what was happening to Tim, and now I was watching my precious boy being plugged up with cords and needles from head to toe.

Tim needed to have a CT scan. During this procedure he had a cardiac arrest. Krystle, Leah and I were waiting outside the radiology room when suddenly the doors swung open and the medical staff were running with his bed.

I paced hurriedly after them asking, 'What's happening? Please tell me, what's happened to my son?' Without answering they entered another room, closing the door. Grabbing hold of one of the nurses, I begged to go in, but she gently ushered me to a waiting room. A social worker came to offer her support, but all I could do was cry and pray. I couldn't get the horrible visual out of my head, that a doctor would walk in any moment and say, 'I'm sorry…'

'Please God, please don't take my son from me yet, I would miss him too much.' At that moment the door opened, I looked up to see a doctor standing there. He began with saying, 'I'm sorry.' My heart sank.

'Your son has taken a turn for the worse. He had a cardiac arrest while undergoing a CT scan. He has a large blood clot pressing on his brain. He is bleeding internally and needs to be transferred to the children's hospital where the professor of neurology will perform emergency surgery. The paramedics are getting him ready now. He has been placed on a life support machine as he is unable to breathe on his own.'

I was in complete shock at this point. I told the doctor that I wanted to see Tim. He replied, 'There is no time to waste.' I insisted on seeing my boy. My precious son was connected to tubes, looking completely lifeless. I leaned over him and kissed his forehead, my tear dropping on his cheek.

I boldly began praying for Tim before he was moved. The doctor explained that if the clot ruptured, the life support machine would no longer be effective to keep Tim alive. As I prayed, every person in that room bowed their head. 'Please Father God, I beg of you, heal Tim, please don't take him from me yet. Restore him in Jesus' name. Amen.'

While I sat in the waiting room when Tim was having surgery, I noticed a Bible on the table. I opened it randomly and read Psalm 41: 1-3:

Blessed is one who considers the helpless; the Lord will save him on a day of trouble. The Lord will protect him and keep him alive, and he will be called blessed upon the earth; and do not turn him over to the desire of his enemies. The Lord will sustain him upon his sickbed; in his illness you restore him to health.

Was God really telling me that he was going to sustain Tim on his sickbed, that he would live? I clung to that hope with all my heart. For three and a half hours Tim was in theatre. Upon return he was taken to intensive care, in an induced coma.

The doctor informed me that he had been required to cut Tim's skull open to release the blood clot and bleeding. He explained that the tube which was drilled in his head was to release the blood. He was not in the clear yet; the next forty-eight hours would be critical.

I remained at Tim's bedside praying and talking to him. Krystle and Leah were still with me. Petra, Tim's other younger sister, had also arrived at the hospital with her father.

On the second day, the surgeon informed me that Tim may have permanent paralysis and would need to learn how to walk and talk again if he survived. On hearing those words, I begged God for a miracle!

The surgeon also told me that there was no point talking to Tim and suggested that I go and rest. 'I will keep talking to him until he responds,' I replied. He smiled at me faintly as he walked away.

No More Tuna Mornay

Just before the forty-eight hour mark, I was talking to Tim while holding his hand. I leaned close to his ear and said, 'Timmy if you can hear me, please squeeze my hand.'

I felt a gentle squeeze, so gentle that I said it again to be sure. Once again he gently squeezed my hand. Bursting with excitement, I screamed out to the doctor, 'He can hear me, he just squeezed my hand! Watch!' The doctor came over to observe as Tim squeezed my hand again. This time the doctor's smile grew wide.

The next day as I sat there helplessly staring at my son, he opened his eyes. Overwhelming relief washed over me as tears streamed down my face. 'Thank you, Jesus,' I whispered.

When Tim first spoke, his speech was normal, other than a very husky voice. After two weeks of being in intensive care, Tim was able to go home with follow-up physiotherapy as his walking was very unstable. Being back home brought its challenges. Tim was having emotional meltdowns, crying a lot. My heart broke to see him like this. I spent as much time as I could playing board games with him to bring some joy into his day.

We had been home from hospital a few weeks when Tim became very ill, vomiting and fainting multiple times a day.

One day I took Tim to a toy store with his siblings. As we were browsing the toys, Tim fainted. I rushed him to the hospital. After several hours of observation he was sent home.

The following day while Tim was in the toilet, he fainted again. I heard a loud thud, rushing to find him passed out on the floor. Feeling frustrated and helpless, I phoned our doctor, describing to him what was going on with Tim.

He told me to bring Tim to see him straight away. While we were in his office, Tim started falling forward. The doctor caught him in his arms as he fainted again. He lowered him onto the floor, proceeding to assess him. The doctor then phoned the children's hospital and told me to drive him straight there. He carried Tim to my car, laying him in the back seat.

Tim had been given a tablet named Phenytoin on discharge from hospital. It was to prevent possible seizures, which can be common in patients who have had a head injury. At the hospital his Phenytoin levels were found to be three times higher than they should have been. He had been prescribed an adult dose, which was why his body had symptoms of overdosing. Tim was again admitted to hospital to be weaned off the medication.

Despite human error, I'm so grateful for God's faithfulness and grace.

And the following year on sports day at school, Tim came first in the sprints!

My Hand in His
Simone Field

'Lord, protect me,' I prayed as I hurried through the dark streets of Miraflores, Lima, Peru. You could never be too careful, you see, here in South America. Having been followed a few times now, I had become quite street-wise in identifying that funny feeling that comes with a person tracking your movements. Turning around in the middle of the street I yelled out loud to the seemingly deserted street, 'Jesus, be my protector!' I saw a man then, hiding in the shadows. He turned and walked rapidly in the other direction at this point, mumbling an insult loudly, 'Borracha…' Drunken woman, me?

I am not drunk, Mr Would-Be-Stalker, far from it. I am not brave either, truth be told. I am just a girl, holding the hand of my God with my eyes shut tightly, trusting that he holds me. I am trusting that his name will conquer the darkness that tries to overpower, even while my knees might be shaking. Turning back up the street, I hurry home, letting out a full breath once I am behind the thick, reinforced, wooden door of my apartment. My husband's job required him to work on a project in a bordering country for a few weeks at a time, which left me here until he returned, to work out a new way of living, adjusting to this foreign culture and language.

Why am I even here? Many would question the logic of it – why leave a perfectly good suburban existence in Perth, Western Australia, to endure 'hardship' here in Peru? To be stymied by rules and regulations alien to me, to not understand most of what is being said around me. To be followed numerous times in the hope I have something on my person worth stealing. Why on earth would we choose this?

It began when, newly married, my husband Garrick and I began to feel discontent with our lives in Australia. We prayed about it, and examined our motives and jobs and then we waited on God. We could only surmise that it was a Spirit-led discomfort as we technically had everything going for us that we could ask for at that point in our lives. So we waited and we prayed and we waited and we prayed some more.

One day, a short while later, Garrick came home and said to me, 'Hey, I just got offered a job in Peru, how wild is that?!'

'Peru,' I replied, 'where exactly is that again?'

'South America somewhere,' was his answer.

We laughed it off and said to each other, 'Can you imagine? How crazy, right?!'

And yet it seemed like everywhere we went after that, this country that we knew very little about, was the buzz word that kept coming up time and again. Not long after the random job offer was declined, we were sitting in the congregation at church, listening to a visiting speaker. Time and time again, he brought up these friends of his who were living and ministering in Lima, Peru. Every time he said the name of the country, I got tingles and little goosebumps broke out on my arms. Garrick and I would look at each other incredulously, our unspoken gaze saying, 'Seriously? This Peru thing again?'

We had a chance to speak with the pastor afterwards and, somehow, that was the conversation that clinched it. We needed to leave Perth and head to Peru. Garrick put out expressions of interest for a job and before we knew it, we had packed up our house, rented it out, stored all our worldly belongings at my parents' house and boarded a plane with a one-way ticket and the promise of a somewhat meagre pay-check from a company we knew nothing about.

I smile as I lean back against the solid frame of my reinforced door. I let my mind drift back over the day I just had. I hardly imagined when we came here, the things I would witness – how today at the medical outreach clinic that our church here runs, I would see impoverished children smiling and laughing. Enjoying life in spite of their dismal surrounds, the poverty that had them in its grip – they were full of joy and thankfulness that we would come out to their village and bring much needed medical care. Was I trained medically? Not at all. But I could take temperatures, triage, play with kids, and sort medications – it's quite amazing how useful you can become when needs must.

And my day job? While Garrick was away and back again many times from our Lima base with his work in geology, I stayed local and worked at a school, teaching in English. In my spare time I took Spanish-speaking classes, ran a dance group on weeknights at my church and helped at or attended that church (in Spanish!) every weekend. While our lives were full, it was possibly the hardest time of our lives up to that point – to stay committed to being far away from family and friends, and separated from each other for weeks at a time.

We stayed in that incredible adventure for two and a half years. Even now, all these years later, having moved back to Australia, with two teenage children, steady jobs and a rich community here – we still talk about how God took us on that crazy, sad, joyful, unbelievable adventure. We treasure the friendships we made there and stay in touch as best we can.

The beautiful thing we learnt from it all? He wants to be with us on adventures like this every day.

God delights in our obedience, he delights when we bring our struggles to him – when we wrestle with the big things of this world, like pain, poverty, brokenness, hardship – and we *still* choose to walk with him. We still put our hands in his, knowing that he is good, he can be trusted and he has great plans for his children.

Musings at a Funeral
Nesta Hatendi

I enter the small church of St Elizabeth with my siblings and other relatives dressed in appropriate black mourning clothes, with the older women covering their heads respectfully. We are in a different frame of mind as the parish priest and congregation prepare to start the service of celebrating the life of my late Uncle Zvidzai. In this modest house of worship which had been my Uncle Zvidzai and Aunt Chipo's spiritual home for some years, the signs of the cross are draped in purple cloth, reminding us that we are still in Lent, a time for reflection and that we should remember we are a people saved only by God's grace. The usual Good Friday services have been set aside to focus on our loss.

The night before the church service, mourners, some having travelled from Uncle Zvidzai's rural home, arrive throughout the night, gathering at his house in town. One woman entered the wake, wailing. People stared at her. Becoming self-conscious, she soon stopped, realising that the subdued crowd, unlike in the rural areas, was aware of noise restrictions in this low-density suburb. No one else joined her; instead, the intermittent singing of hymns continued. Some were already tired, waiting for the evening service delivered with a conciliatory sermon from the priest about death coming to all of us and the need for family unity and redemption. Afterwards, the town dwellers left surreptitiously for their homes, promising to attend the funeral service.

The time and venue of the funeral service had been shared through various media, so where are the mourners? We want to start on time because the graveyard has set times for burials. The church slowly fills up while people converse in muted voices. Some are bleary-eyed, having stayed awake the previous night, keeping the grieving widow company as is our tradition. Soon extra chairs are fitted in the back of the church to accommodate the habitually late.

A hired group of professional male singers drowns the conversations, marking the beginning of the service, as they burst into song accompanied by *hosho* (rattles) and drums while ululating, swaying, and dancing as the spirit moves them. There is always controversy about dancing in the church, but no one says a word as some of the mourners get up to join in. In our different cultures in Zimbabwe, how can you celebrate life if you do not show emotions through singing or dancing?

The male choir keeps the momentum while a camera and video crew move around, committing the proceedings to posterity. They capture the occasion and live stream for those in the diaspora or at home who could not pay their last respects. Some forget where they are as they pose for camera and pictures most will never see.

Although the same priest from the night before had recently transferred to the parish, he knew my uncle and aunt and could speak with compassion about their commitment to their Christian journey and their work to promote the well-being of the church family. He keeps his message simple and straightforward, albeit with some humour, yet reminding us that our short life on earth is in preparation for the hereafter.

During the eulogies, a whole litany of people want to participate. They all speak about the same man, yet he had touched us in diverse ways, both young and old. Our culture believes in not speaking ill of the dead, at least in public. I remember one funeral where a mourning son said his truth about his late father. The two had not got on well. People cast glances at each other, some muttering under their breath whether this occasion was the appropriate place to share such confidential information. What was the world coming to when children could not show respect for the dead? I imagined unflattering comments whirling around: his poor mother, the shame! Can't someone take the microphone from him or ask him to sit down? What was the son thinking of?

In contrast, my uncle's funeral eulogies are respectful and moving, punctuated by intermittent song. Some reflect on his 'timely' death and the honour of having a funeral on the day our Lord was crucified and buried. I wonder how my ashen-looking Aunt Chipo would remember all future Good Fridays. Would they be a painful reminder of her loss, even though Jesus' death resulted in our Risen Lord at Easter?

Aunty Chipo is the last to speak. She looks worn out, having had little sleep and raw with the loss. She narrates about her husband's love and support over 30 years, his devotion to his family, and his not being a stranger to the house of God. Their joint faith had kept them going throughout their marriage's trials and tribulations. She speaks of his deterioration in health when he could no longer attend church, the home visits from the parish priest, his last sacrament of bread and wine, and his anointing with holy oil before his passing in hospital. She shared that his death was peaceful, and he was ready to go. Those who saw him a few hours before his passing could support her testimony. Although relatives were making placating statements in the hospital corridors to her, most had already accepted that his suffering on earth needed an ending.

There are no theatricals or hysterical outbursts from wailers in the church. No unknown disrupters want to have their last say. Any loud displays of grief were for the night before. The shared hugs and pain, the red eyes and muffled sobbing into others' shoulders would go on for some time.

Like others, I am reflecting on my life and death and wondering what relatives and friends would say of me, how I had lived and died. Would I be an example of God's grace? Did I love and want to be loved, or would I be remembered with the bitter words I came across in a March 2023 obituary in the *Adelaide Advertiser*:

Lived 76 years too long. A man who only wanted his 'little ray of twisted sunshine' (narcissistic with a superiority complex) ROT IN HELL.

Such strong emotions from whoever shared these parting words cannot be a source of peace for anyone left behind. I wonder whether our people, especially those from rural areas, feel constrained by the unfamiliar church atmosphere and surroundings. Would they have given Uncle a different send-off where the whole village comes out in mourning, sometimes for fear that others would not provide moral and material support to their families when death came to them?

Soon after the service, a simple lunch is served on the church grounds. Women take off their traditional wrappers, spread them on the grass and stretch their legs under the shady trees as we run out of chairs. With food in their stomachs, mourners are more animated, greeting long-lost friends and sharing consolatory words. No one is ever turned away; some join us while eating, not knowing who has passed on. Hunger removes the shame of joining mourners to get a free meal. The scene reminds me of the biblical story of the man who opened his home to all and sundry because the guests had not turned up for the feast.

People continue to converse before the call to proceed to the graveyard on the other side of Harare. The coffin is placed in the hearse at the agreed departure time. Transport is provided for some through a bus from the funeral home, while others follow the funeral car to the cemetery and divert en route to their homes. They have fulfilled their obligations.

On the way, some are caught in traffic again or get lost and arrive just in time to see the casket lowered into the grave. In the scorching autumn heat, we are the only funeral crowd at the cemetery. Tents for honoured guests are pitched around the graveside, and the overflow is under indigenous trees nearby that strategically provide shade. After short prayers and close relatives throwing handfuls of soil into the grave, the hired male choir and a few women continue singing. Male relatives and friends take turns shovelling dirt and covering the new grave as numerous bouquets, some withering, are placed on the mound.

The end of the burial has come, and the crowd, now more relaxed, slowly disperses, heading for their transport back to their lives. Others take the opportunity to visit the old graves of close family members in the cemetery before returning to my uncle's house and putting closure to the day's events.

A certain peace descends on the graveyard as the caretaker escorts the stragglers out before he locks the cemetery gates under the rays of a slowly setting sun. We gave my uncle a fitting send-off, wishing him eternal peace in his final resting place. We are left consoling family and friends, trying to fill the void.

Help from Heaven
Hazel Barker

Robin, the sole nurse on an oil rig off the coast of Western Australia, heaved a sigh. His duties were to render first aid for the injured. The nearest medical facility could be hours away. Work was tough.

A foreman, his muscles rippling as he slapped Robin's shoulder, joined him on deck. 'So, we'll be losing you tomorrow.'

Robin nodded. 'I can't wait to get back to my kids. These 21-day shifts are demanding, but I'll soon be able to repay the loan on my house.' He yawned. 'Guess I'll head down to my bunk.'

A loud hissing sound stopped him. Sirens screamed. He smelt gas. His mind leapt to the workers. *They'll need me.*

Two oil-drenched men sprang onto deck. A fireball erupted. Flames shot upwards. The rig thrashed about like a fire-breathing dragon. Explosions rent the air. A body landed at his feet. He knelt to feel the pulse. Dead! He leapt up and raced to rescue the survivors.

Fearing the blazing derrick would collapse, men fled for safety. The heat grew intense. Robin licked his lips. They tasted of gas.

The PA system blasted out the dreaded words. 'Abandon ship.'

Some, not waiting for lifeboats to be launched, leaped into the boiling oil-slicked sea, screaming and cursing in foreign tongues. A man staggered blindly, arms held forward. Blood streamed from his face. Robin assisted him and the other walking-wounded into lifeboats.

It took thirty minutes before the first lifeboat descended a fifteen metre drop into the sea. Robin remained on deck. Smoke stung his eyes. He wiped them and gazed heavenward, recalling the time he had nearly drowned when swimming. He had even heard heavenly music and thought he was already dead. God had saved him when his friend dragged his unconscious body from the lake and resuscitated him. Help me again, Lord, he prayed.

Two helicopters hovered overhead. One lowered stretchers. The sound of the roaring fire, the falling debris, the crashing of the waves and the helicopter blades deafened him. He directed men, blackened from oil, to help carry their injured mates. Then he secured the wounded in stretchers.

Ages passed. When all casualties had been hauled up, Robin signalled the helicopter to take off. The second helicopter flung down ropes. Men grabbed them. Tongues of flames licked the air and grew closer. His hair was singed. The heat and smell of burning oil nauseated him. The drumming in his ears beat the rhythm of death. Breathing heavily, he wrapped a wet face towel around his nose and motioned the helicopter to haul himself and the others up.

Robin grasped the ropes. They bit into his hands. Fear clutched at his heart. Grimly, he hung on. The roar of the flames grew louder. Or was it the roar of the helicopter's blades?

Hands reached out to pull him to safety. He gasped a prayer of thanks as he slumped forward and looked down at the inferno.

Help from Heaven

The rig had listed and was engulfed in flames. *Saved again! Thank you, God.*

Piercing the Silence
Jeanette Grant-Thomson

1987. The phone was ringing. I put aside my teaching preparations and hurried to answer it.

'Jeanette.' My sister Arlene sounded distressed. 'I've just had another call from Mum. She sounded upset. She kept forgetting what she was saying and her voice was really weak and nervous. Anyway, she'd locked her keys in the house. She was ringing from her neighbour's place.'

I sighed. Poor Mum. This was about the third time lately she'd lost her keys or locked herself out. What on earth was going on?

'Do you think she's had a nervous breakdown?' I asked Arlene, who saw more of her. I was teaching in Nambour and our family lived in Brisbane.

'It must be. If she doesn't get better soon, I'll take her to the doctor.'

This nervous, forgetful version of my mother continued. When I went down to Brisbane, we discussed it with her. She sat on the edge of the sofa, fidgeting nervously with her beads as she talked. She agreed to go to the doctor with Arlene. I had to return to prepare my pupils for exams.

I rang Arlene every day to see how Mum was progressing ...

Before this, Mum had always been externally calm, a careful person who kept an immaculate house decorated with beautiful home-grown flowers – everything from classical roses to huge fragrant magnolias. An elegantly dressed lady known for her lovely singing voice. As children, we often woke to the sound of our mother trilling through her voice exercises. The whole big Queenslander rang with the melody of her singing.

Then, several years after being widowed, Mum moved down to the Gold Coast. A friend had found her a unit-cum-cottage high on the hillside. We all enjoyed the view up and down the coast and far out to sea. Mum was an excellent hostess to us and our friends, coping cheerfully with her tidy lounge room being transformed into a large dormitory with three or four mattresses spread across the floor when friends came to stay.

She would walk along the beach after a day at work, long blonde hair fastened off her face with a blue band, her hair flying out behind her in the sea breeze. Anyone walking past might hear beautiful soprano notes soaring in the wind.

None of us dreamt she was battling constant fears about her memory while she worked in a secretarial job. She avoided mentioning it.

Then the incidents began. Soon we abandoned the nervous breakdown theory. She was deteriorating, not getting better. We were worried.

She moved to Brisbane to be nearer family.

'Jeanette,' Arlene would tell me over the phone, 'Mum rang me on Thursday. She'd locked the keys in the house again. Luckily, I had a duplicate set.'

'Dear,' Mum would tell Arlene, 'I think I've left the gas on. And I'm over at a friend's place. I can't get away yet. Is there any way you can check it for me?'

Trying to reverse out onto the street, she had backed her little car right off the driveway and into the garden.

'You'll have to stop driving, Mum,' we told her gently, thankful for a clear reason to get her erratic driving off the roads.

She had an MRI and the doctor gave the grim pronouncement: 'She has a degenerative condition called Alzheimer's Disease. The brain apparently shrinks.'

Degenerative! That meant it would get worse. This was the 1980s and we'd never heard of Alzheimer's Disease. So we prayed, asking God to heal her brain. For months we hammered the doors of heaven in desperation. There was no apparent response.

We prayed – often. We wept. We fasted. We discussed Mum's situation over and over again. And nothing changed.

'She can't cope by herself anymore!' we told our friends. We were devastated that neither of us was in a position to move in with her.

'We could move in,' one special couple said. 'Your mother could live in the granny flat and we'd live in the main house. We'd look after her. She'd have her meals with us.'

They did and it worked well. After some months, they bought their own house – one big enough to take Mum too.

The time came when Mum needed full time nursing care. She had become, literally, a full-time job.

After much searching, we found a pleasant nursing home with room for her. The staff were wonderful – efficient and kind. She was happy enough at first and continued to sing, worshipping the Lord in her own little room. She sang familiar songs that most people enjoyed. Her voice was so lovely that staff and visitors alike stopped to listen, even to pray, as her melodies rang out through the corridors.

I moved back to Brisbane to be near her.

As the disease continued to affect her brain, she stopped singing and withdrew to a silent world. On rare occasions she would become upset by any sad news about her old friends' illnesses. Most of the time she simply lay there. It broke our hearts to see her. She'd lost weight so the skin hung from her bones. Skinny, inert, she had all but disappeared.

We would visit her whenever we could, walking through the big front doors and along the wide corridors with their smells of cabbage and meat cooking.

We would take her flowers, her favourite golden chrysanthemums and freesias with the sweet, fresh fragrance she recognised.

'Smell this, Mum,' and we rested the soft flowers near her face. We kept her supplied with a favourite perfume. We set up a tape recorder beside her bed with constant worship music playing. She was so much calmer when worship music played, the doctor actually put it on her chart to have it playing all the time. Fortunately, the other oldies in the room seemed to enjoy it too.

But still she lay there with just the occasional response.

The time came when she stopped all responses and lay on the narrow bed, barely there. The years were passing and nurses began to comment on the number of years she had been in that bed. Grief almost overwhelmed us.

'Will your mother recognise me if I visit her?' her close friends asked.

'No, but it'd be great if you went anyway. I think she senses another person even if she doesn't respond at all,' we told them.

A few went. Most said, 'I won't go then. I'd rather remember her the way she was. So beautiful. So talented.' It was understandable. But Mum lay there, often alone. We went when we could.

We began to ask God to take her home to heaven. She had no quality of earthly life and was a sincere Christian, so we knew that would be her desire. Again we prayed and kept on praying. It was a while since she had made any sort of response to our flowers or family news or even music. We read the Bible to her, knowing she loved it but she continued to lie there, white-faced, unresponsive and still. Silent.

One day I felt God put on my heart a desire to read her Psalm 84.

'Mum, this is Psalm 84,' I began. 'How lovely is your dwelling place, oh Lord …' and I continued through the psalm. 'Blessed is the man who trusts in you,' I concluded.

Mum opened her eyes and looked up at me as if everything was normal! 'Thank you, Nettie, that was just what I needed,' she said clearly.

Arlene and I stared at each other in amazement. Mum had spoken! She had responded relevantly. The Bible was blessing her. She was understanding it as we read, words we assumed went into her spirit, probably bypassing her mind.

'Let's always mainly read the Bible to her,' we agreed. So we took turns of reading her favourite parts, as well as chatting about any family news. We were convinced it all touched her at some level, even when there was no visible response.

'What was her favourite psalm?' I asked.

'Psalm 23,' Arlene replied. So we turned the dog-eared pages to Mum's favourite psalm. 'The Lord is my shepherd, I shall not be in want,' she read.

Mum's eyelids fluttered.

Arlene handed the Bible to me. 'He makes me lie down in green pastures,' I read.

'Look!' Arlene whispered.

Tears ran down Mum's aged cheeks. Her favourite psalm had again reached her at a depth beyond her response to people or the other things she loved. She was continuing to respond at last.

So we kept interspersing our chatty news with her favourite parts of the Bible. She lay there, peaceful and still, but listening, until one morning she seemed unwell and slipped quietly through to heaven.

Uprooting
Kathy Worthing

The news of my husband's job offer interstate was welcome. But I was happy here. This had been our family home for nearly thirty years. Even though our four children were adults now and the youngest was about to finish his last year of university, they had all grown up here. Also, my heart strings were pulled when our youngest said that he needed us there at least until he finished uni. His need for us felt comforting. I have always had strong maternal instincts. So why leave my children? What would it be like to experience 'the empty nest'? Would I be ready when the time came? Would God help me with this transition? Emotional pain and confusion set in. How on earth could I up and leave them? Parents don't normally leave their children. Isn't it supposed to happen the other way around? There were doubts and questions. Oh, and I detest all the work involved in moving. Feelings of instability gripped me.

I had also established my own roots in South Australia with friends, my meditation group, my Spiritual Direction Formation class, the familiar surrounds and the beautiful city of Adelaide which I rarely ever get lost in anymore. So to be honest I had no good reason to leave my comfortable surroundings. I had even begun feeling happy on cold days, which I used to dread.

While reflecting on a poem called 'Stepping into Discipleship' by Valerie De Brenni I found myself relating to the words: 'Returning to his precious nets, he hesitates. To leave them lying at water's edge seems such senseless waste.' Images flashed through my mind of family and friends. The hesitation expressed in the poem resonated with my upcoming move. Feelings of uncertainty and loneliness filled my inner being.

Some months later while in my kitchen washing up dishes I was listening 'randomly' to Christian songs on YouTube. Suddenly, a song by Kristene DiMarco called 'It is Well' played. 'So let go my soul and trust in him' captured my attention. My eyebrows rose as the words rang crisp and clear. In that moment I experienced a transformation of heart and mind. An explosion of joy and peace filled me. There was no conscious decision made on my part. The decision was made for me. My soul felt like it was set free. I could have been an eagle soaring in the sky. Repeatedly over the next few months I sang, while home alone, 'It is Well'. Those words brought such soothing affirmation of peace.

June 2022, and the doubts and fears of moving interstate returned. After sharing those uncomfortable and unsettling feelings with a friend, I found it easier to formulate my fears into words. For example, 'I'm not ready yet to uproot and move. This is going to take time.' Forcing or rushing a feeling won't quicken the desired results.

I wondered what I would say to someone else in my position? 'Umm…Where is God in all of this?' A quiet answer came,'God is in the fear.' Okay, I can accept it. I'm not alone. God is with me! Acceptance and peace settled in. Suddenly there was shifting and positive forward movement again.

Uprooting

One further affirmation that showed me that God was involved in my upcoming move took place in July. The opportunity arose to attend a 'Jesus Creative Retreat' in the Adelaide Hills. What an unexpected joy awaited me. One of the workshops that I signed up for was Liturgical Dance. After a beautiful demonstration by the leader we were asked to break up into small groups. One person from each group was asked to sit on the floor. When it was my turn to sit on the floor something remarkable happened. Dance movements from one of the ladies were extraordinary. She acted out dance movements while walking away from me with her arms held up and stretched outward, freely moving like waves. Then she knelt down with the palms of her hands on the floor and began moving away from me. She lifted one hand slightly and then patted it firmly on the floor then repeated the movement with the other hand. This continued as her hands moved away from me in a straight line.

I was astonished and asked her if she had some insight into what the movements meant. She said, 'As I walked away from you, it symbolised God leading you out and going before you. My hands were feet of peace – a faith path. God is firming your faith – a straight and firm path.'

I realised there are times when God just wants us to say 'yes' and then to let go and allow him to take over. This was one of those amazing times.

Some months later, though more confident in what God wanted me to do, I returned to worrying. Will all be well? How would I feel on my actual moving day in late November?

When the day finally arrived, I awoke with a light-hearted feeling. The blissful feeling was most welcome and undeniably a gift from God. Confirmation. 'Thank you, God.' As I boarded the plane my feelings remained positive. I was trusting God. I kept thinking of the words from Julian of Norwich, 'All will be well, all will be well and all manner of things shall be well.'

As the plane prepared for landing, I wondered how I would feel…

As I approached my husband, my feeling was one of elation; free from doubt, now at peace.

Mercy Mission to Ukraine
Nadia Konik

Prior to the Russian invasion of Ukraine in February, 2022, very few Australians were aware of Ukraine's existence. My husband Robert and I are of Ukrainian descent with family living in Ukraine, and they kept us apprised of the turbulent economic and political situation. During the 1980s, Australian media reported upon Ukrainians queuing for long hours outside of empty shops, unable to purchase basic necessities. We sent regular relief packages only to discover many contents were pilfered before delivery. Some parcels arrived empty.

Then in 1990, just before the dissolution of the Soviet Union, we learnt my Aunt Anastasia was suffering with terminal cancer and unable to obtain basic pain relief. It was the catalyst to pack our bags and head for Ukraine to ensure a safe delivery. The mission was practical, the result was spiritual.

I made contact with a local doctor and obtained appropriate pain relief medications. However, there were many relatives in need and with expectations. The most frequent request was for American brand jeans, sneakers, and double cassette recorders as these high demand items acted as currency. One pair of jeans could fetch over one month's wages and sometimes wages earned were withheld for months at a time. Anything could be sold and purchased on the black market, just not in retail outlets.

Our travel agent warned that Bibles were confiscated and incurred penalties. We planned to carry fourteen, eight printed in Ukrainian and the rest in Russian for the eastern region where the Soviets outlawed the Ukrainian language. All this was a huge moral and logistic dilemma for us, requiring a lot of prayer. We knew we were over the acceptable limits and weights set by the Soviets.

We prayed fervently as our plane landed at Sheremetyevo International Airport near Moscow. We needed to go through customs and then transfer to the domestic airport to continue to Lviv in western Ukraine. After collecting our luggage, we were ushered into one of the custom inspection queues. Our faces shone like red beacons of guilt whenever people glanced knowingly at our luggage. We knew our disregard for Soviet regulations put us at risk. Love for family was our motivation but, in the queue, I began to doubt our wisdom. We needed miraculous intervention!

Gradually we moved along the queue until there was only one young man ahead of us. Our attention was riveted to the procedure unfolding. The customs officer was a middle-aged woman who worked with astounding efficiency. Her fingers probed every nook and cranny in the very small carry-on case until she pulled out two colourful magazines from under the neatly packed clothing. She gasped aloud. 'What is this decadent American filth?' she thundered, and thrust the magazines into the air for all to see. I recognised the type of magazine she was denouncing, having confiscated a copy from my own son when he was fifteen. She must have pressed a button under the counter because two burly, uniformed guards appeared at her side. She let out a tirade of expletives in Russian. The young man paled visibly as the guards gripped his arms and pulled him to one side. The woman raised the small suitcase and tipped all the contents out onto the counter, exclaiming loudly as she did so. Contraband! Smuggler! She located a packet of Marlborough cigarettes which set her off with further expletives and she visibly shook with rage while the poor young man trembled with fear and embarrassment. 'What, our cigarettes are not good enough for you, you pervert?'

Robert and I stood rooted to the ground with shock and terror. Our eyes met and exchanged unspoken words, 'Wait till she sees the contents of our bags!' I carried fifteen pairs of jeans in assorted sizes. There was no way I could claim them as my own. Then there was the issue of the Bibles dispersed between five bags. Two were printed in large print and weighed a ton each. We also carried multiple sneakers and four duty free cassette recorders. There was no way the items could be overlooked.

The customs officer stormed off with the guards and hapless young man, leaving his spilled belongings scattered over the counter. I couldn't help but feel sorry for him. We were next!

The customs officer returned and scooped the young man's possessions back into the case. She turned to eye us without concealing her irritation. It was obvious she wanted to leave with the small bag but we were an inconvenient hold up. She glanced at our bags and grimaced. I trembled. She thrust out her hand and demanded our paperwork, skimming the pages briskly. She raised the official stamp high, her arm lunging like an executioner's sword. Bang, bang, bang! An imperious finger pointed to the exit. We did not comprehend and remained rooted to the spot, ready to hand over the duty free bags. She muttered with disapproval, shoved our paperwork towards us and waved us through. We were dismissed. Again she pointed at the exit and stormed off. It took a moment to realise it wasn't a trap and was, in fact, an answer to prayer. We were free to go with all our contraband and not an item confiscated. We were the last to leave and the most grateful, muttering 'Hallelujah!'

It was Easter and spring time. The rural villages were so picturesque with blossoms and sunshine and scenes from a hundred years back in time. Visitors from outside the Soviet Union were still quite rare, so our presence caused a stir and we were so blessed to experience Easter celebrations with them. (Not a chocolate egg or bunny in sight.) It was the first year under the Soviet Union that churches were freely open for Easter. We met many of Robert's relatives for the first time and we were touched when the Bibles were received with genuine tears, the covers swathed in kisses. People were poor but spiritually rich.

In the villages, the churches were bare except for hand-crafted decorations: embroidery and tapestry depicting Bible stories and Scriptures. People must have worked on these in secret for years earlier. There was a new boldness in asserting their Christian faith, suppressed and underground for so many years. Strangers greeted us with 'Christ is risen!' and the reply before any introductions were made was, 'He is risen indeed!' This occurred in the towns as well as villages in both western and eastern Ukraine. The rumblings for independence had also begun and the blue and yellow flags were displayed boldly when people congregated. Ukrainian television broadcast only Ukrainian folk songs and Christian hymns with the Easter message for three days straight, from Good Friday to the end of Easter Sunday. We were both amazed and delighted. When we entered villages and were ushered to inspect gravesites of relatives, the churches were flung open and people gathered to form choirs to sing to us. In one village, almost the entire population of women and children ran out to join hands in a circle to sing and dance around the newly opened church. We joined the circle and were invited to enter the church where prayers were offered up for us amid thanksgiving and rejoicing.

My Aunt Anastasia lived in Sumy, on the eastern side of Ukraine, and was cared for by my cousins, Vasyl and Shura, who had assisted with paperwork to enable us to visit. A few years earlier they had helped my aunt visit us in Melbourne, where she committed her life to Christ. We did not know then that other family members in eastern Ukraine were part of the Christian underground church. Their children were forced to contend with atheist Soviet schools, particularly in tertiary education. Our aunt asked us to speak with the younger family members who avoided discussions on Christianity. We gladly agreed to her request. We were already feeling buoyant that the medication we'd brought was effective and reducing Aunt's suffering.

Our cousins took us to their parents' village and we met Uncle Petro, my father's double! I presented them with a large print Bible and immediately all hesitance and formalities disappeared. 'If only you'd come a few weeks earlier, you could have joined in with the celebrations. Three people from the village were water baptised!' They challenged their adult children. 'If you won't believe us, believe these educated people from the west.'

My fondest memory is standing in their market garden, from dusk until the early hours with stars and moonlight enveloping us, sharing our faith, the scriptures and answering their questions in our broken Ukrainian. We were a church of seven souls in a remote area of Ukraine, a circumstance I never imagined possible when we boarded the plane on our mercy mission.

My Aunt Anastasia died several weeks after our return to Australia. Now, in 2023, the world is aware of the tragedy in Ukraine and possible global ramifications. I weep and pray for mercy upon the open-hearted people of Ukraine.

Kisses for Me
June Hopkins

It seemed a long time since I had last been kissed. In the thirteen years since I had been plunged into widowhood, with all its attendant emotions of sorrow then loneliness, I hadn't thought much about kisses. I knew I was blessed to have a large family with my children and grandchildren having been nothing but warm and supportive. However, generally, we are not a hugging lot although I easily cuddled them all when they were small. In truth, though, I have never been one to relish touch, especially from those outside my family.

I have been in church services where the congregation has been asked to hold hands across the body of the church while some special prayer request is made. At such times, I can't wait until the prayer is over. No matter how much brotherly (or should I say sisterly) love is felt, I do not like holding hands for a prolonged period with fellow worshippers.

In my family we end phone calls with 'love you lots,' and we express the same sentiment in lovely greeting cards at birthday times and on special days. We spend time together, celebrate events and good times together, even occasionally holiday together, leaving no room to doubt we care about each other deeply. We speak on the telephone regularly, and I enjoy the ability to 'FaceTime' with my loved ones.

Yet, as a now single senior, on reflection I acknowledge that physical touch from people is diminished in my life. It is not something I lament much, so it was that recent events surprised me.

A family circumstance happened that meant my son asked if he could drop his ten- year-old son to me at 7am weekdays on his way to work. My task then was to give my grandson breakfast and supervise him getting ready for school. At 8am I would drive him to school.

It was a return to familiar 'bygone' days as I gently hassled him to put on his shoes and socks, comb his hair, eat his breakfast, and get himself ready for school. It seems there are a lot of modern-day distractions for school children. He has his own phone which provides endless fascination for him, while I impatiently, frequently remind him of the time.

After lots of prompting we eventually get into the car for the ten-minute trip to school.

On the very first day I delivered him to school, he unexpectedly reached for a hug and then gave me a lovely kiss on the cheek. I was surprised by how chuffed I felt as I drove home alone. Since then, this child, with all the normal attributes of a boisterous ten-year-old boy, kisses me goodbye each morning with heartfelt affection.

He has no idea that his simple action makes my days bright and sunny.

Home Remedy
DJ Blackmore

We were babies of the depression, sewn together in the silky dark under cover of the song of the Nightingale Willy.

Swaggies begged any job that was going, and we ate bread and butter with stories of fragmented family. When the sun came up, they were gone again, having left a token stone on the gate post as advertisement for those after some tucker and tea.

A kid didn't count the pennies. And I saw porridge as penitence, pitying myself during breakfast purgatory. A special occasion was when silverside flanked the spuds, at a time when Mum guarded the Coolgardie safe jealously. She usually kept a rabbit in it that the boys had got; skinned, naturally. Surprising how many ways you could cook it. The miracle: it could end up being called lamb roast, served with mint sauce on Sunday.

Fruit was what your granny made into jam, scrounged from bushes nearby. Luckier than some, years ago Dad had planted two apple trees. But like everyone else on our street, the only jam we happened to have was blackberry.

'What do you mean you don't like it?' Mum turned irritably.

'Katy says they have strawberry jam at her house.'

'Her father's a doctor' She screwed a tart face at me.

I was envious of Katy. She got lamingtons and blood plums. Once she invited me around for afternoon tea. We'd had Victoria sandwich filled and oozing with dark pink jam. No sign of any blackberry.

Katy had three dolls that stretched on her bed, living lives like porcelain princesses. I had one, which I'd named Peggy. I loved that doll the moment I saw her, sitting on the top shelf in the store, looking down at me. She had a china face with a body of calico cloth. I'd taken Peggy home and she had stared all the way in the sulky with me.

I had been little then, and skinny. When Dad gave thanks at dinner, he told me that it was only the grace of God that we had something on the table for tea. There were no Iced VoVos at our house. But I knew they ate them at the doctor's place. Pillows of sweetness topped with decadent coconut snow. I'd run my hand over the counter at the store, longingly.

'Fancy people buying biscuits ready-made.' Mum shook her head in wonder, rubbing one of my brother's shirts backwards and forwards against the washboard vigorously. She was sweating like the copper filled to boil the sheets. She blew the fan of her fringe with the bellows of her cheeks.

'Just open the packet and *voila*,' I told her. I was a conjuror clicking my fingers. A bestower of laid-on sweets. 'No dishes to be washed, no cleaning up to do.'

Home Remedy

'Get out and find me the money tree growing between those apples. If you can find it, you're doing better than me.'

The day Katy went down the train tracks to play, I wanted to go too. But Mum grabbed hold of my plaits until Katy got sick of waiting by the front gate for me.

'You're not to go playing around the lines. I'll give you work to do.'

When Katy wasn't back at school, I dragged my feet past there on Monday afternoon.

'You better not come in.' Katy's mum's eyes were red.

'Let her inside,' Katy's dad, the doctor, nodded. Katy's mum always left out a plate of biscuits. I eyed the Iced VoVos hungrily. I ate one and took another, shoving it in the pocket of my pinafore, to enjoy on a greedy walk home before tea.

Before I walked into Katy's room, her father hunkered down in front of me. 'Katy is seriously ill.'

'Too much castor oil.' I nodded. I knew the Friday night remedy too well.

'Katy stood on a rusty dog nail,' the doctor sighed. 'I'm giving her penicillin.' But it looked to me like hope had drained out of his face like water through porridge oats, all white and pasty.

Katy was in her bed. Covered to the waist with eiderdowns and shivering enough to shake the blankets. When my granny went gallivanting, she wore the fur of a grinning fox. Katy's smile was just like that. Stretched taut and ghastly.

I dug out the biscuit I had been so ravenous to take and threw it as far as I could. I came to life, fast as a hare, and ran all the way home.

'Katy's father is a doctor. He has medicine.'

But Mum's smile was tight as she kissed the top of my head. I didn't know about lockjaw then.

'It's not for kids,' was all Mum said when I asked to go to Katy's funeral.

Then the war came, but Dad never went. He found bed instead, staring out the bedroom window, all melancholy.

'Dad's got cancer,' Mum told me like he was at war with the Germans with no hope of return. Like he had shaken hands with Mr Hitler and was never coming home. Tears fell onto her cheeks, scarlet as remembrance poppies.

When a noise came from Dad in the bedroom, Mum would rise with the strength of a one-man platoon. One day I caught her crying and kneeling at the bed. If Dad was going to dodge a bullet, he needed medicine. I knew it.

When school had finished, I strolled on past the store. I went inside and ogled the biscuits, behind shining glass cabinet doors. Then I had the packet in my hand, and I was marching out, as though I had made it past the enemy, with the curative those Iced VoVos had.

'Take Dad a cup of tea, would you, love?' Mum was bent over the copper, hair damp around her temples, face as shiny as a shilling.

Home Remedy

I ran to my bedroom. There under my bed was what I had been hiding. The fancy biscuits that the Arnott family had made famous the whole country over, a panacea for every kind of malady. Mum always said sugar was brain food – so I don't know why she always had to watch over the stuff like it would get up and run away.

'Look what I got.' I dunked a bikkie in his tea. He let me know he was alive by the way he slurped when I held the cup to his mouth.

'This'll buck you up.' I was sure. 'I got them especially.' He just shook his head and turned aside. 'That's why you're so skinny. Seen more meat on one of those rabbits Mum keeps in the Coolgardie,' I tried joking, because that's what he always said to me.

I was reminded of the day I had visited Katy, all stiff as a four-by-two. The biscuits hadn't helped her any more than they seemed to be doing for my dad. He just followed me with his eyes, skin all sallow and shrunk against his skull. Wasn't Mum feeding him? I stormed out of the room and found her in the laundry.

'Forget boiling the linen. Why are you starving my dad?'

Mum opened her mouth to speak then promptly changed her mind. She made a sound as though the wind had been let out of her lungs. She sank to the grass like a damp pile of laundry.

'I stole these from the shop because you never buy any.' I threw the whole packet of biscuits I'd been worrying in my hands. I pitched them as far as I could for the ants. Then I fell down on my knees.

'You think that will cure him?' I was surprised she didn't tan my hide with the strop. Instead, she put her arms tight around me.

'Can't nothing make him better?' I cast around me for a cure. But the garden was empty of my father. It was just Mum and me.

'All the sweetness we can give him won't take the truth away. He's saving strength for every day.'

'There's no sugar in a sunrise!' I cried.

'Not unless it's the last one you might ever see.'

She left me with her words and the biscuits scattered through the garden beds. Then I gathered them up and sealed them. I couldn't let them be thrown away.

At our place after the funeral, the kitchen was spread as though we were celebrating. I took the biscuits out for Dad and for Katy, arranged them just so, in memory. I didn't eat them. They were stale, anyway. But of all the things I learned, it's that life is a lot like a biscuit; sweet until it is gone, and the wind blows the crumbs away. I had thought they had been drenched with the elixir of jam and coconut. That sugar gives strength to the weary. But the Almighty is the only One that sprinkles the grace on our days. And the sweetness of his love costs nothing.

The Voice
Karen Roper

One Saturday morning, my husband and I were eating breakfast and discussing the different activities that we could fill our day with. Some of the suggestions being discussed were, for example, maybe we could go bushwalking, or walking along the beach, or visit one of the children – we hadn't seen them for a while. My husband went to ring his daughters to see if they were busy and they all were.

I went and lay down after morning tea to play a game on my iPhone. It was then that this ordinary Saturday turned into an extraordinary day. I heard a voice say 'Andrew', which is my husband's name. I thought I was hearing things as it is not easy to hear what is going on outside our bedroom. Then the voice came again: 'Andrew.'

I got up and went in search of my husband, now very certain that someone outside was calling his name. I looked in the backyard on my way to find my husband but there was no sound coming from anywhere.

I found him sitting reading his Bible in the lounge. I told him that someone was calling his name. I don't think he believed me at that stage. But I was insistent. It was then I looked out the front window and saw an ambulance parked outside Mr and Mrs R's home. I told my husband, and he came to take a look.

He thought he should go over there, and I agreed. He went over as I continued to watch the happenings at the neighbour's house over the road.

After a while I also went over. When I arrived, they had put Mr R in the ambulance, and I was standing inside with Mrs R. She explained she had had to use the Heimlich manoeuvre twice on Mr R to bring him back to life, as he was choking. She was exhausted from the ordeal and in a great amount of shock. Then she made an extraordinary comment.

'I prayed to the man upstairs and asked him to send me help.'

I realised then that the voice I heard calling my husband's name was God. God was sending her help in the form of my husband. What makes this extraordinary is that Mr and Mrs R don't go to church, but God, in his grace and mercy, had sent Mrs R exactly what she needed at the time.

I was surprised that God spoke to me whilst I was playing a game, whereas my husband was reading the Word of God. This shows me that his voice can come to us anytime; we just need to be open to listening for that still small voice of God. You never know whose life is going to be impacted by you hearing and obeying.

Praying for Princess
RJ Rodda

Our family had to make a serious decision. With the pandemic restrictions tightening, should we stay living in our organisation's ministry centre in the village in the country of Georgia? If we did, we would be potentially isolated from shops, our children's school, our church and friends. Or should we make the move into the nearby city, leaving our dog Princess behind?

Princess had been a part of our family ever since she'd been found dumped with her many siblings at the village school my children attended. My two sons and daughter had heard one of the other puppies had been drowned and they begged us to rescue at least one of those remaining. My husband drove to see them and took pity on the smallest who was very thin and shivery. Her tan coat, white socks, sleek fur and small head with long floppy ears made her attractive to look at but she seemed sick. Would she even survive?

Surprisingly, Princess thrived and grew into a medium-sized dog. She took great delight in racing up and down the lush green mountain we lived on, keeping pace with our car for a long way. Village custom dictated that all dogs roamed free, which was very different from the regulated life dogs live in our home country of Australia. Princess loved running around but was afraid of the other dogs. Before she was desexed, the male dogs of the village would crowd at our gate howling for her. One in particular, a black and white spotted dog named Lordy, was notorious for his uncertain temper. He'd bitten one of the young village girls before and attacked one of our workers but talking with her owner achieved nothing. Princess was terrified of Lordy. We locked Princess up at night in a cage, hoping that would keep her quiet.

It didn't work and Princess's frequent barking interrupted the sleep of our family and the other people staying at our centre who would complain about her. She was not the only village dog barking though and the jackals who had a den on our property also frequently sent their long eerie cries into the night. Since our village was on a mountain near a national park, the potential for bears, jackals, or other animals to be wandering outside meant Princess's noise, while annoying, made me feel safer.

We moved to Batumi, but having to choose in a rush meant we got a modern, nicely decorated apartment that was just big enough for our family and to host the occasional meeting. It was not suitable for our active Princess though. We left her to be cared for by Gela, a young subsistence farmer in our village, and when Batumi went into lockdown we could not visit for a while. A curfew also made it difficult for us to make the trip there and back in time.

When we were finally able to visit, Princess leapt all over us with eager love, even trying to jump into our car to go back with us. This was especially sad for my middle child Samuel, who wanted her to be with us. 'Mum,' he would beg with his blue eyes fixed on mine. 'Can't we bring Princess with us?' Samuel had loved roaming around with his dog in the village and the move to city life had been hard for him.

'It just won't work,' I'd explain over and over again. 'Princess wouldn't like being cooped up in the city. She couldn't stay here.' As I spoke, I pictured Princess restless in our small apartment, incessantly barking, frustrated by the lack of space. I also couldn't imagine our landlord, who was so proud of her property, agreeing to such a big dog living inside with us. Samuel didn't let up though. Tired of his nagging I suggested he instead pray and ask God about Princess.

Samuel stopped talking and started praying…

Really, I knew in my heart I would lose. How could I win against a child pleading with God, especially one so tenacious in prayer as Samuel?

Then after the pandemic ended and the price for our apartment skyrocketed, we had to move. While there was no house available in our price range with a yard, we did find an older, less pretty apartment with a balcony. School holidays hit and my husband suggested we get Princess up from the village and try her in the city. I said yes, because I knew it would make Samuel happy, but I was convinced it would be a failure. How would Princess feel confined to a balcony when she'd had a mountain to run on?

Well, Samuel's prayers worked in a way I never would have dreamed was possible. Princess in the city with us has been a completely different dog. She doesn't jump up, she doesn't bark. She seems content on our balcony and waits for her walk outside to go to the toilet. She's affectionate but undemanding and greatly loved by my children and husband.

Not long after I finished writing this, I got a disturbing text message. Princess had run off from our communal playground and my husband and sons had been searching for her for half an hour. I'd been at a café with my daughter but we left and walked back along the crowded boulevard that hugged the Black Sea, searching for her. We all returned empty-handed.

I asked my tall, oldest son James how he felt about Princess being missing and he said in his nonchalant way, 'I have peace, I guess'. I went outside to search again, and realised that I also felt a peace that it would be okay, that God wouldn't have answered my son's prayer only for us to lose her. Not long after this I found Princess wandering in a confused way next to a small local café/bar on the other side of our row of apartment buildings. With great joy, I grabbed her collar and took her home.

Dad and Jesse
Jenny Woolsey

The claustrophobic blue curtain rustled and a nurse dressed in her hospital navy blues appeared. She studied my face, her eyebrows furrowing. 'Are you feeling sick?'

I blushed and extracted the white thermometer from my lips. 'Ah no, just taking my temperature for my fertility chart.'

I flashed the piece of paper displaying the beginning of a graph drawn with a blue biro.

Her eyebrows danced and rose, she nodded and put her own thermometer to my daughter's forehead. Melissa's soft snores meant she was sleeping soundly, three days post major plastic surgery.

'Dr Arrow, it's been six months and nothing's happening.' I regarded my new obstetrician across the wide teak desk with its colourful model of female reproductive organs and a silver ball hanging in a circle which swung back and forth, back and forth. Maybe it was representative of a woman's biological clock. I had become pregnant quickly, within a month of trying, with my first and second pregnancies and my gut feeling was that something wasn't right.

He bent his head and studied my file. I studied his bald spot. My retiring obstetrician-gynecologist of twelve years had faxed over my medical records. I jiggled my leg, waiting. The metallic circle swung back and forth another ten times.

'All right,' Dr Arrow began. 'You have endometriosis so you might not be able to fall pregnant again.'

'I know.' My foot lifted from the grey office carpet and tapped out a rapid rhythm.

Dr Davis had bluntly stated on my 'I want to have a baby' visit, 'You might not be able to.' But after losing my first rainbow baby at twelve weeks, my home was now breathing with a seven-month-old's cheeky smile and rattly baby toys.

'Fill out these temperature charts and come back and see me in two months,' Dr Arrow said unsmiling, handing me some empty graphs with the Y axis labelled with temperatures.

He didn't give off the warmth that Dr Davis had.

The temperature charts screamed that my cycle was holidaying and out of rhythm. My gut instinct had been correct. I was prescribed a fertility drug and told to keep on with the morning temperature checks before I got out of bed, plotting them on the graph.

'And I want you to have intercourse every two days from day 10 to 18.'

'That's five times a month! Awesome!' Joe, my husband, had grinned at this directive like a straggly malnourished cat that had just scored a bowl of cream.

For six months, the lights dimmed early every other night from day 10 to 18. And at the end of each cycle the appearance of my enemy periods gave disappointment and tugged at my heart strings.

At the end of the next cycle...

'I think I'm pregnant,' I whispered to Joe, after being one day late.

'You could just be late,' he said.

'I feel different, like with Melissa.'

'Do a pregnancy test then.'

In my bedside drawer were two tests hidden in their plastic cocoons, to be unwrapped like a present concealed in Santa's sack on Christmas Day. I removed one from its packaging and stared at the small screen which would soon excite or demoralise me.

Was this a waste of time and money? Shouldn't I just put it off for a week?

I closed the toilet door behind me, followed the instructions as I had in the past, then waited. Joe exited to the front verandah to have his nervous smoke and I paced the hallway. Up and down. Up and down. The floorboards squeaked.

It's going to be negative for sure. But God, please may it be positive!

I snuck back into the bathroom and nervously peered at the screen. My squeal shook the wooden house.

Joe rushed in. 'What?'

'I'm pregnant!' I burbled, shoving the two red lines up in front of his eyes.

'Your father's at the hospital but there's no need to rush.' It was New Year's Day 2003 and my mum was on the phone. 'He had some pains in his chest.'

We ignored Mum's advice and hurried to see him. The half-an-hour drive seemed like ten hours.

Forty-five minutes after arriving, Dad suffered a second heart attack while I was by his bedside having lunch with him, and he could not be revived.

My childhood hero, my support, my protector, my source of wisdom, was gone and I was beyond devastated. One ray of hope kept me going – the baby growing in my womb.

The chatter and yells of students playing on the oval outside the teacher's lunchroom, where I sat, seemed far away. I'd just been to the toilet and found some bleeding. Dread filled my body. Memories of losing my first rainbow baby in 2000 flooded my mind.

'Are you okay?' Emily, the teacher sitting across the table from me, asked. 'You look sick.'

'I think I'm miscarrying,' I whispered, a zap ricocheting up and down my spine. My face drained of its colour and my eyes moistened.

'Oh, do you need to go and see your doctor?'

'I've got my obstetrician's appointment this afternoon.'

Her face warmed and she touched my hand. 'I hope you're okay.'

Dad and Jesse

I went back to the classroom and taught for the afternoon. Somehow, I got through but my mind wasn't with the children… If I was miscarrying again at twelve weeks, there was nothing I could do about it, but I so desperately wanted this baby. This child was my connection to Dad.

That afternoon, when Mum arrived to babysit Melissa as prearranged, tears flooded down my cheeks. I told her my fears. Her hug told me I wasn't alone.

The air conditioning was set on 'chill to the bones' and I shivered as I lay on the hard examination bed beside the ultrasound machine. The jelly was icy and the wand could have been an angry wizard. Two weeks previously the black and white fuzzy image on the screen had displayed a sac, a jellybean baby and a flickering heartbeat.

I dared not look at the screen now.

No one spoke as the sonographer ran the wand across my belly and examined the new picture.

My body turned into a corpse as I turned to the monitor. There was the sac. There was the jellybean baby. But there was no flickering heartbeat.

Oh no! Why, God, is this happening to me again?

The sonographer switched off the ultrasound. 'I'll be right back.'

The next day I presented at the local private hospital to have the baby removed.

I lay pre-op on another cold, hard, white-sheeted bed and stared at the painting of a vase of flowers on the far wall. Joe held my hand. His sniffs filled the vacuum.

'What are we going to call the baby?' I asked him. 'This time I want to name them before they're taken from me.'

Joe nodded. 'Do you want a boy or girl's name?'

We had named our first rainbow baby Lisa after being told at my post-op checkup that she was a girl.

'We don't know what they are. Maybe a name that can be both.'

Dear God, what is my baby's name?

My eyes jumped to *Judge Judy* on the television.

'Look!' I cried, pointing. Joe's eyes flew to the screen.

'That's it! Jesse,' I stated. 'God's just told us their name is Jesse.' I couldn't believe it – the male plaintiff and the female defendant were both named Jesse – with the same spelling.

God had just answered my prayer. He was with us.

Outside the operating theatre, tears poured down my face. The nurse held my hand as I sobbed, 'My dad just died and now I've lost my baby.'

Why God, why? This is so unfair!

An emptiness consumed me on the way home. Once in the house, I hugged Mum and then held Melissa for the longest time. One child of three had so far made it into the world alive.

Dad and Jesse

The next Sunday, I found myself standing in church singing, 'You give and take away. You give and take away. My heart will choose to say, Lord blessed be your name.' As tears welled in my eyes and slipped down my cheeks, I squeezed Joe's hand tightly. In my heart I knew that Dad and Jesse were together.

A week later, Joe poured himself a Coke and asked me, 'Do you want to keep trying?'

I nodded. 'Yes, I do. It's in God's hands whether we have another baby but I would like to keep going and see what happens.'

So, it was back to the temperature checks, fertility charts and day 10-18 early dimming of the lights.

Joe and I could not see into the future and know whether we would have another baby to hold but we hoped and prayed that one day we would.

A Different Kind of Victory
Nadia Konik

We were intimidated by the jarring noise of tanks churning up the road. It was dusk in Moscow, and we'd stumbled across military rehearsals for the Victory Day parade. Soldiers barred our way while we watched sparks discharging beneath the Soviet tanks. The sight was ominous, concluding a day of sightseeing. My husband, daughter and I retreated to our stopover hotel, relieved to be leaving the next day.

The following morning our taxi to the airport was late. Roads were detoured for the parade and we arrived four minutes late for check-in at the airport. At our departure gate the attendant looked directly into my eyes, smiled, and slammed the gate so we could not enter. I waved my tickets but was ignored. Four minutes late, and our seats were already allocated to people waiting on stand-by! Panicked, we scuttled from one airport department to another. We were assured, 'Purchase new fares and take the next flight out.' The over-inflated fares were beyond our means.

We met a distressed American woman forced to sleep in the airport lounge for two weeks since missing her flight. Shocked, I found refuge in the toilets where I howled first, then commenced to pray. Very distinct words came to my mind: 'Pray blessings upon the people you feel wronged you and upon the people of this nation.' That was the last thing I wanted to do, but I had the good sense to obey.

A Different Kind of Victory

I walked back to the boarding gate and saw the woman who turned us away. I wanted to scream at her, not pray blessings, but the Holy Spirit prompting was unmistakable. I began to pray and forced myself to pray blessings rather than focus on our circumstances. Praying sincerely became easier and stress dissipated, making way for tentative hope.

Several hours later we returned to the Intourist office. The officer beamed at us. 'Good news, we have seats for two of you but one will have to remain.' My husband was willing to stay behind but I refused the offer. I returned to the toilet to cry out to God. I was reminded that the Lord fights our battles. I resumed praying with a new dimension of thanksgiving and rejoicing for God's people in the Soviet Union, for the faithful people who love God despite their circumstances. I recognised we were embroiled in a spiritual battle.

We were summoned back to the Intourist office. There were no additional seats found on the next flight but the attendant at the gate had convinced a young mother to carry her toddler on her lap for the duration. This arrangement released the child's seat for our use. We could travel together! God used the lady who had slammed the gate shut to open our way out of Moscow.

On parting, the Intourist officer shook our hands, and said, 'There are godly people in Russia too.' My face coloured. God used him to confirm my lesson. 'We do not war against flesh and blood.'

Solo with God
Ruth C Hall

'Dear God, help!' flashed through my mind as I lay flattened on the floor of my small tent, while listening intently to decide if the gunshots were growing closer. I couldn't help wondering if maybe my friends were right about my idea to go off camping in such a secluded spot on my own. I could just read the headlines now – 57-year-old grandmother shot while camping alone, mistaken for a kangaroo.

Realising the shooting had stopped, I snatched my small lamp from the floor and hooked it up to the inside roof of the tent, then quickly flopped back down to keep listening. I rolled onto my back looking up at the light. Would it be bright enough for the spot-lighters to see? Hopefully it would encourage them to move away from an obvious camper. I knew it was probably only locals out hunting rabbits or maybe kangaroos, even though that was illegal in the state forest I'd decided to make my home for a week.

I stayed put, with my phone held close and began to pray – hard. As the sounds of shooting began again, they seemed to drift further away. I lay with my heart beating fast and thought through how close they may have come; how easily a stray shot could have come through my tent. And the shooters may never even have known. Who would have discovered me? I could have been left there for days! At least the tent was closed up so the blowflies wouldn't have access to my decaying body...talk about finding the positive in everything!

Solo with God

Eventually the shooting sounds stopped. Despite the gentle rustling outside my tent from some small animal feeling safe enough to be back out scrounging for food, I stayed where I was, quietly recovering from feeling like I'd just escaped with my life intact. Wasn't camping meant to be peaceful and relaxing? Not my time for heaven just yet, I guessed.

Many years of, at times, severe depression had culminated in the abrupt end of a relationship with someone I still cared for and which resulted in the loss of accommodation and employment. I needed to just 'get away' from everything, settle my mind and think through my options clearly; to spend time with God and refocus my mind on him. So, with a heavy heart and uncertainty hanging over my head I'd taken off for a week of prospective tranquillity.

I had been camping before, but always with a man around who did all the 'man' things. Despite being a more pragmatic than fearful person, I still felt quite some apprehension about doing this single-handedly, which may also have been based in the general anxiety and trepidation of getting back out there and living life on my own.

I wanted to camp somewhere that I could be quite alone. This wasn't just because I wanted space from people, it was more practical and, dare I say, vain. Being very aware that erecting a tent on my own would be challenging, I was proud enough that I didn't really want anyone watching me. Even though I'd bought the easiest tent to put up (apparently), it actually took me quite a while, but I succeeded.

And that feeling of accomplishment when I had the tent up and my gear organised inside was quite powerful. I stayed for a week and in that time discovered something amazing – I could do this camping thing. Pitch a tent, erect a tarp and a clothesline, cook on a butane burner all on my own. Sleeping alone in a tent in a forest – who would have thought! As the week progressed and I began to feel a certain accomplishment, it dawned on me that, in fact, I wasn't really alone. I uncovered in myself a knowing that God was with me in my alone-ness.

Returning to stay with a friend in Adelaide, I faced an unsure future, but over the next few months a sense of my own personal autonomy under God opened my eyes to new possibilities. Several months later and after much deliberation, I ventured out on my own again. I decided on a road trip to visit my two sons who lived in the diverse states of Tasmania and Western Australia. This worried my loved ones more than my short camping effort because it would involve around nine thousand kilometres of driving – on my own – in my little car – free-camping. Did I mention on my own? Solo? Did I mention it would involve crossing the notorious Nullarbor…solo?

Researching the trip online and chatting to others who had travelled a similar route influenced my decision to go. The first leg was a nine-hour drive to Melbourne. Easy. Then in Port Melbourne I boarded the boat for a night crossing over to the island state of Tasmania. A further four-hour drive brought me to my son Tim's fifty acres of semi-wilderness forest in the temperate Huon Valley.

Solo with God

Seven weeks of living the dream ensued. Well, probably not everyone's dream – but I loved tent life, sharing my space with a mix of wildlife in such picturesque surroundings, on the edge of an uncultivated forest. I needed to put my life back together and those weeks living off-grid turned out to be very healing. My tent was just over the crest of a hill, five minutes' walk to Tim and Tamara's self-contained bus, where they lived with their three-year-old.

I purchased a portable solar-power set-up to keep my laptop, phone and camera batteries charged. Every week Tim carted a big container of water straight from his creek up the hill to my campsite. I cooked on a single burner and kept daylight hours, sleeping when it got dark. I'd go to bed decked out in several layers of clothing with socks, gloves and a beanie – Tassie's weather is basically cold! Often, I would sit outside at night in the moonlight, just observing the abundant wildlife – bandicoots, quolls, bettongs, wallabies, pademelons, and in a nearby pond, even the elusive platypus.

Some evenings I'd venture out on an old track with just my headlamp. What an awe-inspiring experience, walking through the dark in the thick, tangled forest on my own. It was a fusion of beautiful, silent, eerie, mysterious, solitary, serene, delightful and spellbinding wildness – with God in the middle of it.

Those seven tranquil weeks of restoration came to an end, and soon I was on the boat back to begin the second leg of my journey to the other side of Australia, over 4000 kilometres away from Tim's.

This involved driving across the infamous Nullarbor Plain which presented new challenges. The Nullarbor Highway is a twelve-hundred-kilometre stretch of road dividing the rugged coastline of the Great Australian Bight and the arid inland of the Outback. With the occasional roadhouse, no actual towns, remote Aboriginal communities, random wildlife and huge road-trains, I felt quietly intimidated and not a little daunted. But my detailed research had given me no practical reason why I would not be able to do this. I had prayed and sought advice from some mature Christian friends. So, despite my apprehension and struggles with low confidence in myself, I decided to 'Just Do It'. I planned to free-camp in my small tent, taking several nights to get to my son Mike's place.

Some nights, free-camping meant sharing space with neighbours – fellow travellers mostly in caravans or big RVs. Other times I was alone in the desolate landscape that was so different to Tasmania's thick forests. On those nights as I gazed up at the stunning array of stars, I deliberately allowed the stillness and peace of God in the secluded countryside to quell my apprehensions.

Once across the Nullarbor, the last eight hundred kilometres were straightforward. I spent a lovely fun-filled and busy four weeks with Mike's family and my time there was over all too soon.

Saying my good-byes, I retraced my steps home. Taking ten days, the trip back was more of a relaxed meander as I camped in state forests and free campsites. I had conquered the Nullarbor once, so this time the long travel days and isolation were managed with more confidence and self-assurance.

Solo with God

This venture had seen times of self-doubt and misgivings from others. But I did it. I did the whole trip, and I returned a different person in many ways. I still had a future to work out. Still had some depression. Still had to find a permanent place to make my own. Still had to deal with the grief of the relationship ending. But I was beginning to find out who 'me' was. The me that I'd lost for a while was always there, I just needed to be forced in my alone-ness to find myself back in God's arms.

The Night Wanderer
Wendy Zhong

In the suffocating darkness of the room, the stench of fear mingled with the metallic tang of desperation. I stood there, my heart pounding like a wild beast, my breath shallow and trembling. The dim light that managed to penetrate through the tattered curtains painted distorted shadows on the walls, creating a macabre dance of shapes. In my isolation, I had become intimately acquainted with the cold, hard grip of the knife. Its serrated edge glinted maliciously, a silent accomplice to the chaos that consumed my existence. The touch of its razor-sharp blade against my trembling fingertips sent shivers down my spine, a twisted reassurance that I held some semblance of power in this cruel world. The room itself seemed to reflect my own fractured state of being. The worn-out walls whispered echoes of past torment, their peeling paint mirroring the fragments of my shattered soul.

Every creaking floorboard reverberated through my bones, a constant reminder of the weight of my isolation. Lost in the labyrinth of my own pain, I gradually succumbed to the darkness that had swallowed me whole. It seeped into my very being, corrupting my thoughts and transforming my once gentle nature into something far more sinister. A storm raged within, fuelled by years of abuse and neglect, shaping me into a creature of violence – a distorted reflection of the world that had moulded me. I felt my heart beat out of my chest with rage. I could hear my heartbeat in my ears. I was filled with this burning anger. My mind was going a hundred miles a minute with thoughts of revenge. I was so mad that my hands were shaking. The heat of anger was making my body sweat and heat up. But amidst the desolation, a sliver of light pierced through the cracks of my desolate existence.

You entered my life, a beacon of warmth and kindness. Your words and actions offered respite from the shadows, a glimmer of hope that I had long thought extinguished. With each interaction, you chipped away at the armour I had forged, peeling back the layers of my wounded heart. In your presence, I discovered a world beyond the torment, where trust could be earned and kindness was not a luxury but a fundamental right. The power of your compassion and acceptance resonated deep within me, thawing the ice that had encased my emotions for so long. Through your friendship, a long-forgotten desire awakened – a yearning for connection, understanding, and a love that transcended the scars of my past.

The knife that once was my saviour became a relic of a darker time, its purpose overshadowed by the gentle touch of your hand, which reminded me of the strength and beauty that lay within me. As the years unfolded, we walked the path of healing together. Though the wounds of the past would never completely fade, they no longer defined me. With you by my side, I learned to embrace the light, to rewrite the narrative of my life. And with each step we took, the darkness of my past lost its hold, replaced by the warmth of love, acceptance, and the profound gratitude that bloomed within my heart.

Let the Children Come to Me
Cherie Love

We have been babysitting our six-and-a-half-year-old grandson since he was around five months old. What wonderful, fun times we have had in building a beautiful relationship together.

My son went to church regularly until he was about twenty-one years old and his wife has never been a Christian. I have therefore had to be quite careful in sharing my faith with Caleb because his parents have made it quite clear that I can't talk about 'God stuff.' The odd conversation, a few Christian stories; nothing much really in the grand scheme of things.

But seeds grow when planted in the right soil.

A few weeks before Christmas we were doing our usual stint of babysitting in the school holidays, when up piped Caleb, telling me the whole gospel message from the birth of Jesus up until his resurrection.

My mouth dropped open for a full ten seconds.

'How do you know all of that? I've never shared that with you!'

'Ohh! YouTube. Or maybe TikTok.'

'Whaaat?' I couldn't believe my ears. 'Did you go and look up God?'

'Yes,' he replied innocently. 'On my tablet.'

I am sure that his parents have some sort of parental lock on his tablet, but he is very mature for his age and I don't think that they monitor what he is watching too closely because they trust him. Caleb explained to me that 'he watches two guys telling stories from the Bible.'

I decided to cover my bases with my daughter-in-law and relayed the conversation to her.

She wasn't too fazed, which was good. 'Oh, he's interested in a whole lot of different things.'

We left it at that.

This year we decided to pick up Caleb from school on Friday afternoons so that we can spend more time with him. We figure that he won't want to do that in a few years' time. He really is the most delightful child, and it also gives my son a few hours break until we drop him back home. My son usually gets home in time from work to pick him up, as he starts quite early, and his wife takes him to school on her way to work.

This year, Caleb has been sharing all his learning with me, normally when my husband is out of the room. (He is a not-yet-believer). It is as if Caleb knows that he can talk more freely to me when no-one else is around, and I am not sure that he has told his parents any of this either!

'Nanna, do you know that if you believe in Jesus you will go to heaven, but if you don't, you go down to hell. I want to be a good boy so that I go to heaven!'

One day he excitedly shared another story with me. 'Do you know that a girl died in the Bible and Jesus brought her back to life?'

'Yes, that is right,' I exclaimed. 'Are you still watching those guys talk about God?'

'Yes! I love learning about God, Nanna,' he said, snuggling up to me.

We have these little conversations every now and then. I normally let him broach the subject and answer his questions as best I can. I still find it quite unbelievable that he is so interested, given his non-Christian home life. They are brilliant parents, don't get me wrong, but like most Australian families, God doesn't get into conversations very much, except as a swear word!

'You can ask Jesus into your heart if you believe in him,' I ventured one day.

'Whaaat? How does he get inside your heart? He won't fit in there!'

'Well, he just kind of does.' I laughed.

The next week, Caleb really blew me away. We began to talk more about Jesus and Caleb wanted to know about his daddy. Had he ever had Jesus in his heart? I explained that he did, when he was about Caleb's age (probably younger) but that he didn't think about 'God things' anymore. Maybe he had forgotten about him.

'No-one is going to take Jesus out of my heart,' he declared stoutly. 'He's going to stay in there.'

To say that I was absolutely overjoyed at hearing this is an understatement.

'Well, not everybody believes in Jesus, so don't you let anyone talk you out of it. Everyone is different and they believe all sorts of things, but you have the truth in your heart now!'

'No, I won't, Nanna.'

We sometimes underestimate God. We hear of Muslims all over the world having dreams of a 'man dressed in a white robe', and they are saved by Jesus, and of course we rejoice in that, but do we believe that he can work in the hardened hearts around us? In our homes and in our neighbourhoods?

I have worked in primary schools as a chaplain for fifteen years, and I can tell you, with great sorrow, that most children have never been taught about Jesus. Some of them mentioned belief in 'the Universe' or some other tenet, and some stated that they don't believe in God at all. But many children told me that they believed in Jesus, even though they never went to church.

I did not think that I had said much to Caleb about Jesus while he was growing up, and yet those tiny seeds somehow sprouted in his little heart and grew into a beautiful tree. Who would have thought that a six-year-old would google Jesus?

I can't wait to hear of Caleb's latest adventures in learning about God!

Learning to Ride a Bike
Roslyn Bradshaw

Carol didn't own a bicycle, but she knew kids who did. Her friend Bev, for one. Bev's home behind the general store was full of delights, including a cubby house, with a huge box of clothes for dressing up. You could pretend to be a princess, or a pirate, a ballerina or a cowgirl. There was an enamel miniature tea-set, a play oven and even a play cash register. They spent hours playing together during the holidays. Bev's two brothers preferred sword fights, cowboys and Indians, and bike riding. They flew away on their bikes, riding them in circles and showing off. Bev could ride, and Carol really wanted to be able to ride too.

One day she asked if she could try. The younger brother said, 'Sure, here.'

'What do I do?'

'Just put your leg over, push your foot on the pedal, and off you go.'

She grasped the handlebars and pushed on the pedal. The bike moved down the road, wobbled dangerously, and fell to one side. She was suddenly flat on the ground, with the bike on top of her.

The boys laughed. She rubbed a scrape on her shin, got up and tried again. *This time I will hold the handles straight,* she thought.

The bike careened. Bang! It fell to the other side.

'You have to balance,' said Roy.

'Show me how,' she begged.

Learning to Ride a Bike

Bev got on and rode down the road with barely a wobble. Carol watched her intently.

Again Carol tried, and again she fell off. *Ouch!* One last time, she tried, leaning the bike against a post before she launched out pedalling furiously. After six turns of the pedals, wrenching the handlebars back and forth, once again Carol and the bike were on the ground.

'I have to go, thanks.' She limped off, hiding her embarrassment. A scrape on her knee stung, and her eyes stung with tears.

Now and again, Carol would try to ride Bev's bike, but her spirits sank each time.

I just can't.

Don't give up, you can do it, said a voice in her head. *Keep trying.*

One day, when she started pedalling, the bike hardly moved. It seemed to be standing still in the sand, but miraculously, it was staying upright. The wheels turned really, really slowly, and Carol stood on the pedals and held it upright, gripping tightly. She sat back, reversing the pedals to brake, and stepped down.

Bev's mother came out and said, 'The tyres are flat. Bring it here and I'll pump them up.'

When Carol got on the bike with the tyres pumped up, she felt more confident, remembering how to hold it upright, and as the bike took off, she adjusted her weight. She rode the bike to the end of the lane with the barest hint of a wobble. She turned it around and rode back. Her eyes shone. Her heart pounded, and her legs whirled resolutely round and around.

I can, I can! I can ride a bike!

That night in bed, Carol thought about the flat tyre. It seemed like God's answer to her unspoken prayer.

'Thank you,' she whispered.

A God-Given Glitch
June Hopkins

My daughter looked at me sideways with a wry smile. I waited for what she was about to say.

'Mum, we think you are probably on the spectrum,' she offered, perhaps expecting me to react negatively. I merely smiled at her because the thought was not unfamiliar to me. I knew she meant the autism spectrum since yet another of my grandchildren had been diagnosed recently, making five out of my fourteen.

I've gradually formed the conclusion that there is a glitch in the family with various expressions of autism able to be identified even a few generations back. I traced my genealogy as a hobby from the age of fifteen, discovering some related individuals had been regarded as 'hermits' a hundred and fifty years ago. Fortunately, there seems to have been a writing gene at work over generations as well, and I am privileged to have a memoir written in 1923 by a great aunt. In her record she describes several relatives as taciturn, dreamers, reserved, withdrawn or different. I suspect that maybe they were somewhere on the autism spectrum also.

My dad was highly intelligent though he was only educated in a bush school to Grade Three. A loner who loved to read, he was a fount of knowledge regarding the night sky. As children, standing in the dark beside him, necks craned to look upwards, we were fascinated to have him share so much about the stars. Was it a fixation? I saw his encyclopaedic knowledge as something to be admired.

'Why do you think I'm on the spectrum?' I ask my daughter who has two children diagnosed.

'You're always fascinated with numbers, you like collections of things, [I collect money boxes, thimbles and puppets], you don't like groups, you don't like touch except from family, you like writing, you're very organised, you write lots of lists…'

I interrupted her accurate description of me, prepared to defend most of these statements as 'normal' activities. I decided not to fight my case though, because I had known for a long time that I was a bit 'different.' Undertaking a course in psychology as a young adult, I took the Myers-Briggs Personality questionnaire. I showed up as type INFJ. (Google to learn more about the test). INFJ describes only two percent of the population and has the smallest number in the sixteen identified categories. I was enlightened as to why I 'clicked' with so few people. Over the decades since, I have repeated that test a few times and always arrive at the same category. This type is rare because they hold a unique combination of traits including introversion, intuition, good insight into people and situations, and are thoughtful nurturers, yet they like to be independent. They usually have a few deep, strong friendships but not many casual ones. On the downside they are sensitive to criticism, they overthink things and over-analyse, they may appear aloof, they insist on planning everything, and they may have social anxiety. Many of these traits might today be described as belonging to the autism spectrum disorder.

Within my immediate family, the grandchildren on the spectrum are intelligent, clever, and creative. Most are high achievers at school. They all tend to have difficulty joining friendship groups although each has at least one special friend. They like rules and their personal integrity is admirable. They tend to love facts and individually can inform me in extensive detail about things like frogs, the Titanic, particular films, and such. One had speech issues as a toddler, both expressive and receptive. Therapy wrought wonders and he now excels at school despite some residual language difficulty. Another only had five words until age four but, as a teenager, now has good verbal skills. One has sensory issues with clothing being the source of most difficulty – too hot, too cold, too loose, too tight, too smooth, too wrinkly. It requires patience and thoughtfulness to address the problem.

I love each of these grandchildren and am proud of them. I don't see their autism as significant because each is fearfully and wonderfully made in my eyes. I can't imagine them any other way. I am expecting them all to be successful in life.

My favourite chapter in the Bible is Psalm 139. These verses reassure me that God created me and his works are wonderful. His thoughts about me outnumber the grains of sand in the world. He is with me. He perceives my thoughts. He is familiar with my ways of doing things. Before I learned to speak, he knew me completely. All these statements found in the psalm are truly mind-boggling.

If my possible autism is a 'glitch', it is one that God gave me. Autism is often described as a neuro-diverse or different way of being rather than a disorder, even though children on the spectrum may need help with specific functions. Today, some parents of children on the spectrum choose to be neuro-affirming, meaning they endorse the differences and help their child reach their potential as the person they were born to be. This is how I treat my grandchildren.

Meanwhile, I love my collection of about three hundred puppets, many of which I made. I reflect happily on years as a young mother when I had a puppet theatre and entertained kindergarten children. These days I lend the puppets out to schools and children's ministries. I enjoy solitary pursuits such as writing, and I enjoy my own company. I also love conversation and outings with long term special friends. My fascination with numbers doesn't mean I am good at mathematics! I've always liked to know how many of anything – people at a function, items in a bargain, the hours required to do something, etc. One other example of this trait is my need to have round figures in my bank accounts. I will transfer odd amounts such as twenty-nine cents to make certain the balance in an account ends with zeros. Perhaps it's quirky but it has its benefits.

As a Christian I think of the autism traits in various family members as being God's glitch. It's a good glitch. He made us and sustains us, and loves us just as we are.

Throw Your Heart Over the Fence[1]
Helena Stretton

It had been a very stormy night!

Power lines were down, trees uprooted and creeks were flooding into homes. Not until morning did I discover the neighbour's very tall magnificent Silky Oak tree (*grevillea robusta*) had a large bough hanging precariously from high up, the tip of it, on its way down, having smashed the corner of the garage that supported solar panels. A State Emergency Services team was called in to complete the bough's fall and thus make the area safe. However, soon after, to my surprise, the owners called in an arborist and had the tree removed altogether! It is always a sad occasion for me to see a mature tree cut down, and even more so when it is an Australian native. It had probably been planted the same time as my backyard Silky Oak and my other neighbour's one likewise! To lose one had made an obvious gap in the attractive forestation of our backyards which had given much welcome shade in summer and spectacular bright orange florets of flowers in the spring. They then attracted a range of beautiful birdlife, including flocks of chattering, colourful rainbow lorikeets.

But to my alarm, the sadness soon extended when the neighbours on the other side of me decided they would remove their Silky Oak also for safety reasons! What is more, I was shocked when

---

1 Title: Words from Norman Vincent Peale: 'Throw your heart over the fence and the rest will follow.'

they indicated that I should do the same with mine. Oh no! As a tree lover I felt the pain of such a suggestion deeply. Did I really want to agree and comply with such an idea?

My tension was enhanced by the fact that when I first moved into the area over ten years earlier, I had known no-one and sought to build friendships with my neighbours through hospitality and the organisation of evenings in my home. When, after a couple of years, the group had extended to eleven people of all ages, I planned a summer neighbour walk together at dusk, viewing the stained glass around the front doors and windows of ten houses in our nearby streets. The owners of the houses cooperated by turning on their hall lights to enhance the viewing of the windows' beauty from the street footpaths. We didn't need to go on to private property at all. The group ended up at my home for supper that evening where they could view my small stained glass window across the top of my front door and continue their excited chatter. Clearly the group had enjoyed being together.

After our Covid lockdown years, we celebrated being able to come together again by meeting with our chairs and a table under trees in a nearby park for afternoon tea. Children had playground equipment there to enjoy and adults had plenty to catch up on with one another. But a highlight was the award-giving time for everyone, for we could work out some specific action or difficulty that all seven households had faced and overcome during that restricted time, facing hardship or illness with fortitude and positivity, in one way or another. Sharing in this way built our bonds together even more.

So how was I to face this unwanted decision from them to remove my tree, the largest of the three? And worse, the arborist's grubbing machine for removing the roots would not fit down my house driveway. The neighbour then generously offered to remove a section of our common fence so the machine could get through. I knew then that I would have to cooperate with my neighbour's request for the tree's demise and just accept the emotional and expensive loss. Besides I had no wish to unsettle the strong neighbour bonds that we had developed over some years now. These were all my friends. And so the third Silky Oak was taken down.

However, further testing came when it was time to return the fence to its original state and I realised the fencing material had been buckled by the tree's roots. New Colorbond fencing panels would have to be purchased. I naively assumed that this would be a shared project but not so according to my neighbour. It was my tree that caused the damage, so it was my responsibility totally to fix the fence. Besides, he was far too busy to fix it for me. He suggested I go online, having first taken photographs and measurements of the buckled fence and gap, and get some quotes. This was all a new experience for me, so a matter for prayer and then I tentatively proceeded. I had no answers to my first three advertisements but with the fourth I received a quote for $1595 for materials and labour. My neighbour called it a rip-off, but others said that in our current climate of shortage of tradespeople I may well have to pay this price. So what to do?

Next morning my neighbour phoned me. His wife (from a large Italian family) had said to him she did not think I should be left to pay the bill myself and so she was going to contact her brothers to see if they would help with the labour. What a woman! The outcome? Yes, I need only pay for the materials, for which the bill was $375! I was totally amazed and humbled, and thanked the family involved profusely, and God for his wonderful provision.

On reflection, I do not think this would have happened had we not shared our lives as neighbours over many years. I think Norman Vincent Peale's words are probably true. And, more so, it reminded me of the power of prayer once again and the generous grace of God 'to do immeasurably more than all we ask or imagine' he would do for us! (Ephesians 3:20). What a God!

Kindling
Steph Penny

I awoke struggling to breathe.

Strike-a-light, I thought. This cold is getting worse. I'll have to call in sick.

I rang the doctor for a medical certificate. What a nuisance, I complained inwardly. I had no idea this nuisance was about to rapidly descend into madness.

'Hey doc, I have a cold, I'll need a medical certificate for today.'

'You don't sound well,' commented the doctor. 'Can you count to twenty in one breath?'

'Sure.' I'm a singer. I have great breath control.

I got to eight before running out of air.

'Come in and see me right now,' said the doctor.

'But aren't you fully booked?'

'I will make time for you,' he insisted. 'I'm concerned about your breathing, and I may yet have to send you to hospital.'

I suppressed the urge to groan. Oh no. Not another trip to hospital.

I live with chronic fluctuating illness, ranging from mildly annoying symptoms to full-blown, life-threatening flares. I have spent an awful lot of time in hospitals. I'd be happy to never see an Emergency Department (ED) again.

I went in to see the doctor. My vitals were fine, but I was still struggling to breathe. He recommended I go straight to hospital.

I let out a sigh. 'But what if it turns out to be nothing?'

'It might be nothing, and they might discharge you. But it could also be micro-embolisms. And I can't take that chance.'

Drat. He was making sense. My illness carries a high risk of clots, and doctors are always worried about missing a clot somewhere.

I reluctantly went to hospital.

I quickly noticed how bad the shortness of breath was. I couldn't walk very far. I kept stopping to recover my breath. The walk from the car to the hospital entrance was a long one indeed.

I told the triage nurse what was wrong. 'Shortness of breath,' I panted. 'Also chest discomfort and wheezing. And a recent cold.' They pointed to a chair and I sat down to wait, gasping for breath. I felt like I had run a marathon.

Breathing problems will get you seen pretty quickly. They took me in and started running tests. They asked about my two-day cold. 'It was a normal cold,' I said breathlessly, 'and the COVID-19 test came back normal.' They did another COVID-19 test anyway, which was also normal.

They admitted me to the cardiology ward. They took my blood which was normal. The chest x-ray came back normal. The clotting and heart attack markers were stunningly normal. They ran several echocardiograms which were – you guessed it – normal.

At one point, I went for a short walk down the corridor, turned around and walked back to my chair. When I sat down, I could hardly get my breath. I felt nauseous, my head was pounding, and according to eye-witnesses, my face went bright red. More terrifying than that, my airway felt like it was closing off. I couldn't breathe.

I alerted the nursing staff who immediately threw medication at me. I tried to regulate my breathing, but it was thirty minutes before I felt normalish. That was the scary point. After that, it was frightening to walk even short distances for fear of my airway closing off again.

On the second day, the cardiologist discharged me. 'I can't do anything more for you,' she apologised. 'Go back to your GP and do further tests as an outpatient.'

The match had been struck. I didn't know then it would spark five months of madness.

My GP ordered further tests, all of which yielded normal results. One week passed. I realised I was not going back to work anytime soon. The medical investigation was ongoing and until I had a diagnosis, I could not get treatment, let alone return to work.

For the next few weeks I had a medical appointment every day. (Luckily, I was off work.) I was referred to multiple specialists and arrived at their rooms severely out of breath, panting my details to the receptionists, and almost begging the doctors to help me. None of them could explain why my tests were normal with symptoms so extreme.

My GP's tests got more specialised with each passing week. He methodically worked through various hypotheses and ruled them out. The lung scans with contrast came back normal – no clots. The heart scans came back normal – no functional problems. Asthma? No. Chronic obstructive pulmonary disease? Nope. We tested for long COVID-19. The brain MRI was normal. The neurologist ran tests for myasthenia gravis (a degenerative muscle disease that can affect your breathing), which was normal. Repeat bloodwork came back normal.

Three months passed. Then four.

I was beside myself. Not only did I feel thoroughly guilty about being off work without a return-to-work date, I was terrified this problem would never be diagnosed. I had a sense of dread this would never get better.

This is my life now, I told myself. I'll be permanently disabled by this. I'm going to be medically retired at forty-one.

I don't care how strong or resilient you are. That's frightening.

I prayed continually. I prayed for answers, for the doctors, for my workplace. I prayed for God's comfort, for emotional stamina, for spiritual endurance. But God seemed strangely silent. He shared no insights, clarity, or promises. He simply sat beside me, enduring the same madness I was enduring. I was glad for that, but frankly, I was annoyed too. The flames of illness were blazing – and there was no firefighter in sight.

The longer God stayed silent, the more I got fed up with him. In the end, after months of daily praying, I stopped. I could no longer rehash the same old problems. Prayer had reached saturation point. I was done – not with God, but with speaking to him. Silence became my prayer.

Bless my doctors, they kept trying. My pulmonologist (lung specialist) sent me for a lung exercise test. Somehow I got through that exercise, feeling like I was going to vomit or pass out. But they found something: my heart rate skyrocketed, hit its threshold quickly, and physically stopped me from continuing. We had a partial answer: my heart was to blame.

Still, no one could tell me why. I went to a third-opinion cardiologist who arranged a cardiac MRI. It was awful. I mean, worse than the lung exercise test. They gave me contrast to drink which made me want to be violently sick everywhere. I had to hold it down for three hours, get a radioactive injection and wait another hour. I was tossing and turning on the bed, chewing ice chips and anti-nausea pills, willing the contrast to stay down. I dashed to the bathroom to take care of what was coming out the other end. Then back to bed, writhing uncontrollably with stomach cramps.

Finally, they did the scan. It took ten minutes. I went to the bathroom afterwards and vomited everywhere. They sent me to ED. After a couple of hours, the symptoms backed off and I could travel home. I figured the ordeal would be worth it if the scan showed something.

It came back normal.

Where did that leave me? I was disabled by breathlessness, unable to work, sing or talk. I had a heart problem but doctors were unable to pinpoint it. I had no diagnosis, no treatment plan, no trajectory for recovery. Oh, and no hope. I had run clean out of hope. My life was consumed as though by fire, burned to ashes.

All I had was grace. God stayed with me and gave me grace. I wasn't holding on by a thread anymore. He was holding me.

Then, at five months, my doctor noticed I was talking more easily. My sentences were slightly longer. My recovery time was a little faster. We kept an eye on it, and slowly, slowly, things improved of their own accord.

My doctor theorised this Madness-Without-A-Name would resolve around the six-month point. We experimented with a return-to-work plan. I began working from home on reduced hours and light duties. Over a period of three months, I worked my way back to normal hours and normal duties. My body was healing.

But my mind was not.

I was permanently affected by this experience. I faced the prospect of losing almost everything because of a cold and an unnameable complication. I sat in heavy mystery for almost six months, no hope, no healing, no answers. I am still terrified of getting another cold and restarting the nightmare all over again.

Kindling

My mind and faith are not what they once were. But perhaps that is not all bad. Perhaps my body has been kindling for some kind of fire, and in the aftermath, something new and green may rise out of the blackened remains.

The future is mystery. I only know that my God, who sat with me in the inferno, is good at persuading green things to grow again.

I Have Plans for You
Alison Short

I had been tracking a particular work group for opportunities which would advance my career and professional growth. When an opportunity arose it was off-site – in Canberra – which was a three hour drive away from my home. So much prayer, discussion and discernment went into deciding what to do. In the end, I felt that God was giving me an opening that I needed to pay attention to. My family and husband were supportive. However, this was still a time when it was acceptable for a man to go away to work but not so acceptable for a woman. I heard so many stories of people telling me I would lose my marriage, and many people thinking we were splitting up. One plus was that I was able to be back home at least one long weekend a month. My husband and I often deliberately had lunch together at his work to reduce rumours and misunderstandings.

It was tough living alone again. I had to negotiate a rental agreement, gather sufficient goods for living comfortably and deal with fuses, garbage bins and crickets. And it was cold – Canberra! Through the initial ups and downs, I wondered whether it was all worth it, as I struggled to negotiate new geography and new friends, and to get used to my new work situation. I vividly remember one cold morning driving to work, feeling disillusioned and dispirited. And then it came to me, the still small voice of a Sunday school text: 'I have plans for you, for good and not for evil, that you may have a future and a hope' (Jer 29:11). Suddenly, life changed – and I knew I was where I was meant to be. The uncertainties faded away.

Not only was I able to share discussions about my sense of meaning in life with my colleagues, but I later had an opportunity to join the ecumenical Christian Meditation (WCCM) movement in Yarralumla, in time co-leading a new meditation group starting in Curtin. It was always a talking point with my new colleagues that I could even *be* silent for twenty minutes! In laughing about this, I had opportunities to express my faith to others. At the same time, joining the Christian meditation group gave me great personal benefits in deepening my faith and understanding. This supported me through an intense period of several family disasters, so that I could keep on with problem-solving and avoid my threatening full-on panic, since I needed to remain the strong one for the whole family.

Much later after my two-year stint in Canberra, this initial bible verse remains precious to me and is on a plaque hanging above my home office computer, and the silent prayer of Christian meditation has informed both my theological studies and writings, as I continue to seek to put together God's ongoing will for my life within the context of his world.

Baby in the Bathwater
Morton Benning

There's an old saying: we make our plans and God laughs.

We were surprised and impressed how much support we received from the midwifery group, and were excited about bringing this new tiny person into the world, but when we told other people about our plans there were always people saying, 'in the end, the important thing is to have a healthy baby.' I couldn't deny it was true, but it always felt as if they were preparing us for the inevitability that our plans would all go wrong, and that felt unkind.

Getting closer to the expected date, the doctor informed us that the baby was stuck at a weird angle, with her head under Jess' ribs on one side, and her bum on Jess' hip on the other, which explained the odd angle of the baby bump, and the extreme discomfort Jess had been experiencing. They tried to turn the baby, but she wouldn't budge. We were informed that 'this baby will not engage on her own, and intervention would be necessary.' We were told we should book a C-section.

This felt disastrous, but we held on to hope that things would change. We prayed and asked God to help the baby turn so that we could go ahead as planned. We discussed it and decided that we should book the C-section for the expected due date to give Baby as much time as possible to turn on her own so we could cancel the procedure and revert to plan A.

She didn't, and we couldn't. Apparently, God wasn't so concerned about fitting in with our plans.

Our first daughter was born by C-section on her due date, a little too close to Christmas. My wife had to lie on a table and have a great deal of medical intervention. We stupidly opted to leave the hospital prematurely, not really knowing anything about the effects of surgery, and Jess had to deal with a lot of pain as a result. It took eleven days for Jess' breast milk to come in – I presume because her hormones hadn't aligned to the fact that the baby was on the outside now, and exceedingly hungry. We had to see breast feeding experts, but Jess persevered, and Talitha[2] eventually got properly fed. We had a healthy baby girl and that was what mattered. We begrudgingly conceded that to be true.

When our second baby was coming, Jess became anxious about how things would happen. It was suddenly very hard to get support for the water birth Jess had wanted. After a C-section, doctors become very nervous about the possibility of a tear in the scar. When we started talking about minimal intervention our hopes were met with much graver expressions. The midwifery group were not available to us following the prior C-section, and we found it very hard to make headway with our plans. We would not be allowed to use the water birth room in the hospital nearest to us, and people

---

2 Named for the tender Aramaic phrase *Talitha Koum* 'little lamb, get up' in Mark 5 when Jesus raised a little girl from the dead and then instructed her parents to feed her.

were very reluctant to agree to many of our requests. They advised us to consider another C-section or at least expect that medical intervention would be necessary and should be in place as early as possible. I'm not sure if I could possibly overstate how much Jess was opposed to that idea.

One day Jess broke down and openly wept on the phone to someone about being allowed access to a room with a bath at a different hospital that was well outside our zone, and eventually someone put us in touch with a doctor who would be supportive and help us with a VBAC (vaginal birth after caesarean). We made our plans and accepted all the conditions and prepared for a second attempt. The doctor walked us through all the risks and helped us establish a plan we could agree to that would allow Jess the best chance of a very low intervention birth in a bath. We signed a lot of documents to say that we had been properly informed of risks and had agreed to an acceptable plan.

It was eleven o'clock at night and Jess was already two weeks past due. She had been having irregular labour pains for a couple of hours when we contacted the hospital. They told us to come right away. We sat in a small room all night while Jess continued to have contractions, nurses came in occasionally to check progress, and no one seemed very interested in the details of our carefully crafted plan. They just left us to wait.

In the morning we were taken to the birthing room and eventually Jess was allowed to get in the bath. Finally things seemed to be going according to plan. After a while a doctor came in to talk us into allowing a number of medical interventions that our carefully constructed and pre-signed plan had been made purposely to avoid (until absolutely necessary.) I was astounded that she had the gall to tell my pregnant and actively labouring wife that we were putting her in an 'uncomfortable position.'

Then, disaster.

There was meconium in the water. This was one of the conditions under which Jess would not be allowed to remain in the bath. It meant the baby was in some distress. Suddenly nurses were getting Jess out of the bath and putting her up on a table and asking about various types of intervention that would be required. No one paid much attention to our plan, and they started arguing with us about accepting risks (which we had already signed off on in the plan they were ignoring).

Annika[3] was born mid-morning and mid-year. She was almost overwhelmed by the deluge of breast milk which had, by now, been long accustomed to the feeding requirements of a voracious three year old. We had another healthy baby and that was what mattered.

Apparently, God had a similar opinion to the nurses about our plans.

When our third baby was coming there was very little support. Apparently, we were old hands at this sort of thing now, and though

---

3 Nordic variation of both Hanna, the Old Testament mother of Samuel the prophet, and Anna the only named prophetess in the New Testament. Two women who waited and trusted God to give them what they longed for.

concerns about tearing C-section wounds were much reduced, it was unlikely that we would be able to get access to the special room again. We contacted a friend, Bonnie, who is a doula (a little like a midwife, but more accurately described as a non-medical childbirth coach and advocate). But when Jess was a little over a week past due, we were bracing ourselves to deal with some very familiar conversations about necessary medical intervention. We were pretty sure Baby was going to come in the next day or so. Jess' mum was prepped and waiting for a call to come and mind the older girls when they woke up in the morning. Things were still going roughly to what remained of our plan.

On the final night, at about 9pm, Jess went to have a bath and relax herself and I went in for an early night, hoping to get a few hours of sleep before what I assumed would be a stupid-o'clock-in-the-morning call to drive to the hospital. At around 10pm Jess called me from the bathroom to tell me to call Bonnie as she was having contractions and wanted her advice about whether we should go to the hospital now. Bonnie said everything was probably fine, but she would come shortly. As soon as I was off the phone with Bonnie, Jess was calling me again to ring for an ambulance because Baby was coming right now.

While I was on the phone giving info to the ambulance folks and opening the door to let Bonnie in, Jess was in the bath giving birth. She delivered the baby all by herself without me even in the room. Bonnie went in to see Jess and the baby, and the paramedics arrived soon after to cut the cord.

Baby in the Bathwater

Phoebe[4] was born quickly and easily, both she and Jess were fine. We had another healthy baby, and Jess finally got a water birth, but not quite how we had planned.

Apparently we make our plans and God laughs, and then he says, 'Wait till you see what I have coming.'

---

4 Named for the first person to preach the book of Romans to its original intended audience.

The House that God Found
Barry Horner

I felt like Scrooge – unwilling or unable to even contemplate change. Yet my heart told me we needed to shift house. We were retirees and the landscape around us had changed markedly.

Sprawling suburbia had long devoured a once rural location. Earlier days had seen us picnic at the end of our road. Today it's a busy intersection with a regional shopping centre.

Once tranquil market gardens opposite were now packed with houses and their domestic din. Our road that had led to pastoral serenity now carried endless streams of cars to their destinations, punctuated with the screams of emergency sirens. Add a nearby school and you have a twice-daily, self-imposed retreat while parents drop off, and pick up, their children.

Beyond environmental concerns was our progressive inability to cope with general house maintenance and block size. We needed something smaller and quieter.

A friend introduced us to the world of real estate. Weekends were quickly immersed in viewing prospective houses. We learnt the language that ostensibly described these houses. A purchased laser-measure checked the often-imaginative room sizes shown in brochures.

The House that God Found

Our established routine lasted over two years. This would be our last house. We had to get it right. Family and friends gave advice: 'You'll need to compromise' and 'You'll never get exactly what you want!' Were they overlooking the God factor?

We both held a steadfast assurance that God had a place for us. He knew our hearts' desire – a house given to hospitality, where people of all ages, with diverse backgrounds, would come and eat, fellowship, and – oh, did I mention coffee?

I frequently analysed our financial position, often none too quietly. We needed to choose wisely. If we got it wrong, our capacity to 'correct' a mistake would be minimal. We were at the wrong end of the age spectrum to rebuild our finances.

Experience made us quite adept at predicting a house's selling price. Indecision saw the odd house slip by. Twice we were significantly outbid. Clearly the buyers were more desperate for the houses than us. We continued to feel God's affirmation.

As we journeyed we became aware of a few, just a few, prayer stalwarts supporting us. The market seasonally ebbed and flowed. Weeks could pass with little to view. We became familiar faces at inspections and would occasionally get asked our needs and be placed on a list.

One sunny Sunday afternoon my wife Jenny drew my attention to a house in a location I had ignored. We arrived at the address and immediately noted the adequacy of street parking, and the general flat terrain.

Once inside I soon sensed a 'feeling' about the place. There was nothing outstanding about the design *per se*, but everywhere I turned, my eye would come upon some endearing feature that reinforced the warm glow rising inside me.

To the rear was a well-designed and sizeable patio with an outside kitchen. This shouted 'hospitality' to me. Jenny, too, was progressively ticking boxes. She looked composed, but I could see she was smiling widely on the inside.

We contacted our children and a friend. The next day they joined us for a follow-up inspection. This house was a serious contender. But there was a problem. It had no actual price, just an invitation for offers.

Based on our experience, we lodged an offer. It was rejected, but within days the house was given a price range. We marginally extended our bid, remaining significantly short of the top price.

Bids closed and the agent contacted us. Our price had been accepted, albeit reluctantly. The owner's lack of enthusiasm reflected the trifling interest shown in the house and the urgency to sell. It was then I learnt that, while seeking the Lord's guidance on prices, Jenny had been praying that if this was God's house for us, other people would show little interest in it.

We shifted house. Four months later our old house went on the market. It sold at first inspection during a 41°C-day. The sale price exceeded our expectations. Indeed, the extra money matched the stretch made to acquire our new house.

We've heard of 'the house that Jack built'. Well, we have the house that God found.

The Heart of a Midwife
Esther Cremona

Pauline read quietly to the baby who lay in the humidicrib beside her. Her voice provided a soothing reassurance for the sleeping infant – a boy – who had been born ten weeks premature. He was only a few days old and his little form lay serenely, his breathing soft and regular, a naso-gastric feeding tube providing life-giving sustenance. No oxygen supply, no heart monitors constantly beeping, and no paediatric specialists checking in. Nursing staff were in short supply in the busy hospital.

The gentle and essential touch of Pauline's hand lightly stroked the velvety down of hair on the precious head, the sensitive skin of the little arms, hands, legs and feet. The baby had turned his head towards the lull of Pauline's calm voice, his little toes wiggling and pale pink fingers flailing to grasp and hold onto Pauline's hand.

The baby and Pauline were the only occupants of the basic, but warm, hospital room in Karachi, Pakistan. Pauline, a qualified nurse and midwife, was the infant's sole medical support, and human contact, for much of each day. The baby's father was a missionary doctor, and after a full day of providing essential health care for others, would arrive to care for his son overnight. At night-time Pauline would eat, drink, shower and partake of some hours of sleep. The infant's mother was unwell and unable to be with her baby in the first few weeks of his life.

The Heart of a Midwife

Pauline hadn't planned on being in Karachi to care for a neo-natal infant. She had been serving in women's health in Pakistan for several years, based in the town of Multan, over eight hundred kilometres away from the bare room in which she now sat. She had travelled to Karachi to seek counselling from an Australian psychiatrist, for her despair, her unsettling feelings of insecurity and creeping depression.

Back in 1980, Pauline believed God had called her to Pakistan, to care for women's health, in Multan's community. With her nursing and midwifery qualifications, together with genuine compassion for helping people, Pauline cared for others across various – and numerous – circumstances. During scorching summers, she worked in roasting temperatures that reached up to 46°C for several months. Pauline came alongside women with much-needed comfort as they experienced painful miscarriages, and witnessed the heart-breaking passing of young children, their small bodies unable to cope with severe sickness. She gently persisted in implementing safe birthing practices, praying to reduce the high mortality birth rate.

With the limited resources available in the mid-'80s, Pauline served within a team of missionaries, passionate about teaching women safe health, hygiene and birthing practices. A number of young women in the Multan community were also keen students, spending two years training with the missionary team Pauline served in, to become midwives in the community, local villages and hospitals.

Pauline was actively involved in children's ministry. She volunteered to assist in teaching adult literacy to eager students, most aged between 12 and 17 years of age. There were obstacles for some of the girls, as their household chores and caring for younger siblings were expected to take priority, but Pauline and her comrades persevered with the students when they were able to attend. Pauline bonded with many of the locals, and one such kinship meant she was invited to be a bridesmaid in a wedding. She was delighted to join in the wedding preparation and celebration for her friend.

Yet Pauline experienced a nagging gloom that shadowed her incredible ministry. In letters to a dear friend in Australia, she wrote, 'I still have great difficulty believing that I have anything to offer here' and 'it's like pieces of a jigsaw puzzle that haven't come together yet.'

One particular night, when the murkiness threatened to occupy Pauline's core, she picked up her guitar, wanting to worship and cry out to God.

But she couldn't.

A blanket of wretchedness covered Pauline, and sorrow seized her heart. She didn't know what to do, where to turn or how to disentangle from such despair. Pauline sobbed and implored God, 'Help…I don't know what to do!' Tears coursing freely, she turned to her Bible, and God guided her to a passage from Romans: '*the Spirit himself intercedes for us with sighs too deep for words.*' Pauline's prayers questioned: 'How does my heart heal? It hurts so much'. God shepherded Pauline to chapters from Ephesians, encouraging forgiveness, letting go of resentment, urging her kindness and compassion for others. Pauline's sadness didn't come between her and God, it was the moment that God held her close and began to heal her heartache.

Pauline's faith was unshakeable, but still her blue feelings were deep and restless. Sleep became a haven for nightmares and she sought practical guidance from her supervisors in the mission compound. Mid-year 1986, she embarked on a train ride to reach Karachi to receive help from a psychiatrist.

Through her sessions with the doctor – and much prayer – Pauline recognised that feeling under-valued and dejected were related to lifelong hurts that her heart had clutched onto for many years. Combined with an astoundingly virtuous, but challenging, ministry of the past few years, Pauline had lost her sense of her own self-worth, and how treasured she is by God *and* people.

She would return to Australia in December 1986, after serving two three-year terms as a missionary, midwife and nurse in Pakistan. But there was one other vital role God had assigned to her. Pauline was sought after by the family of the baby boy, born ten weeks premature. They had heard not only of her integral skill set, but also of her compassion and genuine care for others. The baby needed Pauline. It was God's way of saying, 'My dearest Pauline, I have a precious child that needs you. I'm blessing him with your compassionate care.'

For three weeks Pauline blessed the baby boy with her practical care, devotion and heart-felt prayers. When the baby's mother was well enough to finally hold her son for the first time, Pauline felt privileged to be alongside at the tender-hearted moment.

Shortly after her time caring for the infant, Pauline did return to Australia. Although she has still experienced moments of doubt in the shadows, she unwaveringly trusts God during the dark and tough times. Pauline remains humble, but her faith-filled strength and compassionate ministry shine a light that is unmissable.

Dagger in the Heart
Jo Wanmer

A dagger in the heart of my life-dream. A death blow. The letter was very clear. There would be no children – all hope of five children gathered on my knee dashed.

There is little to say, even to each other at those times. Tears were pointless. I looked for a way forward.

'I'll get adoption forms tomorrow.' I kissed my husband and went to bed. I did pray for a miracle, for God to overcome this barrenness, then I bundled up my broken heart and pushed it into some unseen hidden recess, and erected 'Keep out' signs.

Being the early seventies, the wait for adoption wasn't prohibitive. Within four years we had our gorgeous little boy and a precocious baby girl.

Life was full. Full of laughter and tears, nappies and cute outfits, challenges and joys. Yet every month marked another disappointment, another non-miracle. I struggled to re-corral my unreasonable, illogical heart. *I am a mother. I am blessed with beautiful children.*

Both babies had been over three months old when we first cuddled them. I grieved the loss of the newborn experience, the birthing process, the little person made in our image. Firmly I squashed that wounded heart back into its hole.

During a huge national conference in the mid-eighties, they offered to pray for those who couldn't conceive. I jumped to my feet but my husband's hand stayed me. *It's too late, we're too old, the kids are too old.* As I watched crowds stream to the front, my tears escaped. My broken heart, jerked out of hiding, now demanded attention. I sobbed throughout the last two hours of the meeting and all the way home. I cried as our friends prayed for us and held us. Exhausted, I slept, but that hidden broken heart was heard and that allowed healing.

God's healing was complete. Months passed without a miracle, without pain or sense of loss. Peace replaced angst.

Then the Lord started to restore to me all that was lost.

Over a period of ten years, I assisted with the birth of six tiny babies. I watched as squished heads morphed into faces. I waited and rejoiced over that first breath. Eight grandbabies flooded into my heart and arms. What a God of extravagance.

Yet he had one more gift for me. My granddaughter brought her brand-new baby boy home to live at our house. For the first time, early every morning, a newborn was in my arms. I watched him stretch, grow and develop. I monitored every little change, covered him with love and kisses.

When he moved out, I was content. He was just over four months old. We had adopted our son when he was four months and eight days old. This little one lived with us for exactly the same number of days. Every day I'd missed of my son's life, God had returned to me. He filled the last little cracks in that broken, battered heart with gold.

Classic Road Trip
Roslyn Bradshaw

I'd always wanted to visit far north Queensland, but it is so far from Adelaide. It takes a lot of time, money and incentive to get there. Even when all of those lined up, I found there could be other obstacles to face.

We had an SUV and a caravan, and a plan to spend two months on the road, stopping at every cove and forest, trekking to every waterfall and landmark, with the luxury of an empty nest, air conditioning and an ensuite van. We were going to escape South Australia's cold wet winter as well as avoid the high humidity of Queensland's summer.

Ah, the freedom, the adventure, the relaxation. What could go wrong?

As was our custom, we prayed before leaving Adelaide. We prayed for protection for us, for our car and for others on the road. Manangatang was to be our rendezvous, but when our travelling buddies weren't there, we called.

'Hi. Where are you?' I asked in a worried voice.

'We got to Bordertown and the van had a flat tire. We're nearly there.' Sure enough, they soon pulled into our parking spot by the old railway station.

'Lucky we set out early,' my brother-in-law said. 'I got out the jack, and it was too tall to fit under the axle. I'd never used it before.

Obviously for an off-road van. The factory must have made a mistake. So I called the RAA and they had the right jack. Then we had to replace the shredded tyre.'

'At least you got here safely, and you can use our jack.'

As we spoke, a semi-trailer pulled in alongside us, then another one, and another. Massive rigs kept arriving until 11pm and started roaring out at 3am. I slept like a hibernating wombat, but my brother-in-law was awake all night.

The next leg of our journey was up the Kidman Way, an old stock route. The main item of interest was the Black Stump Hotel, with the highest bar in the Southern Hemisphere, said to enable you to enjoy a drink without dismounting from your horse. It was a dizzying climb up the stool. When we stopped, the men's attention was diverted by the disappearance of the vented cover for the plumbing taps on our van. They scavenged a plastic storage basket, cut and glued it to shape and affixed it with Alien Tape, the modern successor to the all-purpose duct tape of the 1980s. This was the first of many running repairs.

Moving on, having decided that 400 kilometres was enough to drive in one day, I found a lovely-looking camping spot by the Lachlan River at Hillston in the Camps book. When we got to Hillston, we stopped to google it.

'Oh no! No signal!'

Ask a local, I thought, seeing a police station across the road. Perfect! I strode up to the closed door and checked my watch.

4.30pm. They should be open. I knocked. Then I saw the sign: 'If this station is unattended, please use the telephone on the wall to call — — —.' I called and listened to the phone ring, and ring, and ring. Eventually, a young woman answered. I explained our predicament, and she asked, 'Where are you?'

Where are you?!

'Hillston. Can you help me?'

'The police station responsible for Hillston is — — —,' she replied, naming another town, 'but perhaps I could help you. However, this phone will cut out after five minutes. Don't worry, I won't have cut you off.'

I wondered what would happen if we had a real emergency requiring police assistance. Is this what life in a remote country town is like? Fortunately, she was able to give me directions before the phone line went dead, and we found our quiet, picturesque camping spot.

In the morning, we were tempted to stay another night, but we had a deadline, a surprise 80th birthday party for a sister in Brisbane. On we went, past Cobar to the 'back of Bourke.' We camped on a patch of red earth where the temperature dropped to 2°C at night. We side-tracked to Lightning Ridge to soothe aching joints in the 43°C artesian baths, and to noodle unsuccessfully for opals. We crossed into Queensland and continued across the bucolic Darling Downs to Toowoomba where night-time temperatures hovered above zero, arriving in Brisbane to their coldest and rainiest winter for years.

Our niece warmly welcomed us to her Wamuran property.

'What happened to sunny Queensland?' we complained.

It rained every day and every night that week, but we had our party and family time, mostly spent in heated shopping centres.

It was time to set out into the unknown, up the Inland Way to Port Douglas. We had no set timeline, no bookings and not even a fixed route. All four of us agreed that we would relax and take it one day at a time, going wherever we felt led. A serendipitous meeting with a woman in the toilets at the Duaringa service station was the first such lead. I noticed that her companion wasn't responding to instructions.

'Is she your sister?' I enquired.

The woman nodded, exasperated.

'Sometimes it's hard,' I commented sympathetically.

'Where are you headed?' she asked.

'Emerald.'

'I'm from Emerald.'

'What's it like?'

'Not bad. We have everything: supermarkets and even a Bunnings. Say, if you're going that far, go to the Gemmies.'

'Gemmies?'

'The Gemfields. It's 15 kilos past Emerald, and you can fossick, or just buy a bag of wash and see what you find in it.'

Classic Road Trip

It was a highlight of the trip to find thirty shards of sapphire: green, yellow, black and blue, hidden in a bag of dirt. Many other locals helped us find hidden gems to enjoy along the way.

We may have had SatNav to help us plan and navigate, but it was an uneasy relationship. Approaching the Mossman Caravan Park, the cultured voice of the navigator instructed 'Turn right in 50 metres.'

No caravan park was in sight. We went around the block in convoy to try again.

'Turn right,' she intoned again.

As we complied, we spotted a park sign to the left, but it was too late. Around the block we went again and turned left.

'You have arrived,' the SatNav said.

As time went on, we learned to judiciously ignore SatNav advice, for example, when she tried to send our caravans down muddy, single-lane roads just to save a few kilometres.

Soon the weather was warmer, yet our sleeveless tops remained packed away, and I bought a new pair of jeans. We loaned our rellies an extra-warm quilt. Often it poured at night, leaving the ground around our caravans a quagmire, and we draped the washing under the awning to dry.

Where was sunny Queensland?

One bright spot was the Innot Hot Springs, where I read a book in the sunshine after soaking in their warm pools. Even on our cruise to the Barrier Reef, my husband wore his cardigan and I snorkelled wearing the stinger suit more to keep warm than anything. The Daintree Rainforest was a fascinating verdant tumble of vegetation, but not the steamy jungle we expected.

From Cape Tribulation we headed slowly back down the coast, sailing in the iconic Whitsunday Islands, meeting kangaroos on Cape Hillsborough Beach and tracking down wild crocodiles at Babinda. Whenever possible, I swam. I bravely plunged into swimming pools, mountain rapids and waterfalls. What about the beach? No way! There were warning signs everywhere. 'Danger, crocodiles. Do not swim' and 'Danger, stingers.' There were even signs about which stingers could kill you.

What could go wrong? Everything!

Back in Brisbane, we finally found the sunshine and donned shorts and sandals for outings with the family. At night we put the heater on, noting it was still warmer than freezing South Australia. It was tempting to head north again; however, we had things to do at home. So, with mounting urgency like horses on the homeward run, we decided on a familiar route south. We'd had enough adventure.

At home, narrating our adventures, my vial of shiny sapphires reminds me that God is in control of all things. It's a matter of vision. Our prayers had been answered. God had kept us safe during our 10,000-kilometre trip. That errant semi-trailer didn't run us off the road, we had had no accidents and hadn't even needed our first aid kit. At times our experiences seemed like an unappealing bag of dirt, but within were hidden precious gems of blessing. And that's life, as my Auntie Dorothy said when we visited her in Karoonda on the last day of our road trip.

Fighting For Life
Val Russell

Life is one big fight that, for me, began over sixty years ago. I fought to be born, to be loved. I fought for hope, for justice, acceptance, and value. Did I find it? I found Autism. I found strength, devastation, an empty heart. I found out I was different in lots of ways. People tell me jokes they find hilarious. I try hard to work out what is funny. I wonder why they don't tell real jokes. I would watch people admiring how clever they were. Seconds later, I would feel like an alien, a creature that didn't belong in their world. I would try to sink inside my skin hoping I was invisible. I must fight for truth. I am autistic and that is okay with me. I am completely unique.

Thirty years ago, I sang a song I wrote, at my dad's funeral. I sang what I wanted him to know but could never say while he was alive. As I stood before my family, I willed myself not to make a mistake. People needed to know I had ability, that finally, I could do my dad proud. I concentrated hard, then became lost in my song, my personal goodbye message to my dad, so surreal. It was sad, but I didn't feel sad. What was there to feel sad about? Death occurs constantly, it is a fact of life. I was just disappointed that I didn't feel important to my dad. I told him how much I longed for him to talk to me, craved for him to hold me. He didn't. I couldn't cry. Crying was a concoction of frightening emotions leaving me feeling sick and terrified of being alive and alone. The day my dad lost his battle to cancer, I lost all hope of belonging to anyone. I wonder, did he hear my song from heaven? Did he know how much I needed him? Was he smiling or was he sad?

I had tried so hard to please my dad in every possible way, thinking that would help him to love me more, but I didn't understand that pleasing others doesn't work. I know he loved me in his way, but in the depths of my mind, I was still his dumb daughter. The one who consistently failed at school and, as a teenager, couldn't hold a job for long. I thought, 'What is wrong with me?' I wish I could tell my dad: I have completed four degrees and can hold down a good job. Would my dad be pleased? I think so. Would that cause him to hug me? I think not. It was not his way.

The challenge of communication never ends. Emojis on text messages? Makes no sense to me. I can never identify any except the basic ones. To avoid making a fool of myself, I only use a smiley face. I am challenged to show or label emotions. Well, other than anger. That is the one emotion I don't want to show. I prefer to lock it up which has become my superpower. I can go anywhere I like and no one would really know I have autism. It's my secret invisible life only I need to know about. On the outside I appear relatively normal, on the inside I am fighting for life, trying to cope with everything while masking, wishing I could be who I really am. Ah! My anger. I am a patient person, but pushed too far and I can snap when alone. Then my hands feel like tiger's claws ripping apart its prey. So strong, powerful, the energy of a roaring fire destroying everything in its path. Within a microsecond the object I am holding is flying across the room, usually my phone. Amazingly, I haven't broken one yet, probably because I am rarely alone. In the presence of others, the anger goes into my dustbin, hidden under the mask, but when alone I am the one in my anger's path. The power of the tiger's claws can turn into a self-destructive rage. Acting out violent anger is not okay and leaves me feeling God cannot love me because I am so bad.

'Why are you changing my routine?' I want to ask but cannot. Changing my thinking and my way of doing something appears to me to be an impossible feat. Like banging into a brick wall repeatedly. Who would do that when they can walk through the gate a metre away? Change means facing failure. It means I am not important to you. Change is a total inconvenience and I need a few moments of peace to process it before I can respond appropriately. I let the emotions, the anger, of course, subside. Taking a deep breath, I tell myself it will be okay. Tears usually prick the edges of my eyes and I try to blink them away, so no one sees my reaction. I don't cry. Only babies cry. Processing the change requires me to tell myself that people are not against me. I have not failed again. I need warning of change. I become very angry and feel unimportant when change occurs suddenly. I have to pull in all the strings of my emotions, so they don't drag me down. Panic sets in and I feel unsafe.

I am a sensitive soul. I hurt a lot when others are hurting, but I don't know how to respond. I know God loves me, but I struggle to feel his love. Amazingly, God still thinks I am a good person. Makes no sense to me. Doubtful thoughts rise from the depths of my being. They need to be confronted by the truth. I feel guilty and think God is disappointed in me. I know he is not, but I still think he is. I need to make a huge paradigm shift in my thinking and in the essence of who I am. But how? Can I change my brain? My environment? Filling my brain with truth instead of lies means changing something. But change equals fear. Catch twenty-two.

I have learned to trust a few people in my life, but why is trust so hard? Sixty years later, I am still fighting this battle. What is wrong with me? I needed my dad when I was a child. I never felt safe. One thing I have learned in the last few years is that anxiety, lack of trust, panic is the result of fear. Fear means I don't trust God to protect me. I likened my fear to being in the middle of the Atlantic Ocean, alone, treading water to stay alive. Will someone find me? Do they even know I am alive? How long can I survive? There is a movie, *Gravity*, where people are floating in space with no means of getting home or being found in such a vast atmosphere. Watching that man drift into nowhere was terrifying. No, wait, worse than terrifying! 'It's just a movie,' I hear you say. Not for me. Maybe fun to watch for some but leaves me terrified. Fear goes deep. What will happen when the world ends? When Jesus comes again? Who created God? I cannot dwell on this fear, it is crippling and unbearable. It means I don't understand God's love for me because love casts out fear.

My dad was so incredibly smart. I felt like the dumb black sheep of our family. I was wrong! I am intelligent too, just like my dad. I've even seen the brains in my head! I have successfully brought up three beautiful daughters. When they are unwell, I feel bad, like it should be me, so it is not them. After one week of being a mum, I was ready to give my daughter back. What a shock to my young mind, to care for someone else. Strange unfamiliar emotions filled my body, and I could not understand them. I searched everywhere for answers in the handbook on raising children, but never found the right answers. Did anyone know what I needed to know? I was trapped in a world I didn't understand with no family support close by and no internet. Forty years later, I realised I had succeeded in being a good mum. I am so very proud of my super-intelligent and loving children and grandchildren.

Autism is not an excuse for lack of achievement. It has never prevented me from reaching my goal. It has made life difficult and challenging behind the scenes, but God has my back. I'm not sure that everything he wants to teach me is what I want to learn, but I love him anyway. Knowing that God is on my side I continue fighting for a super good life.

God is Our Provider
Cherie Love

'What are we going to do?' moaned my husband.

We were in a bit of a ditch, to say the least. My husband had had shoulder replacement surgery a couple of months before this, which meant he needed to have about six months off work, but we hadn't been worried, as Barry had a sickness and accident insurance policy. They would pay – right?

After about nine weeks of haggling, we gave up on ever being paid by the insurance company. They kept denying our claim, because 'it was a matter of wear and tear' and not an injury. We should have read the small print!

At the end of this time we were both exhausted and a bit defeated. I was a born-again Christian but my husband was not. The future loomed ahead of us like a deep dark tunnel threatening to engulf us. Barry had always worked for himself, first as a carpet layer, and then for many years as a courier. Of course, his shoulder had deteriorated during his many hours at work! Year in and year out, he would only take about ten days off for holidays. Maybe a few extra weeks off would have helped, but who knows? Severe osteoarthritis ate around his shoulder joint like an avaricious predator seeking a victim. I guess that is how we both felt in the beginning, like victims.

I soon learnt that the Lord was about to unfold many miraculous provisions during the next four months. We had to go on Centrelink for the first time in our lives, but it really gave me an appreciation of how tough it is to live on benefits. What a blessing it was to live in a country that practised social welfare. I was a chaplain in a school, and they miraculously gave me another day's work. Unheard of!

Another miraculous provision during this time was that an anonymous person was sending us cash in the mail once a fortnight. This helped greatly, as our younger son was at university and our oldest only worked part-time. With all of these little surprises and blessings, my faith began to soar. We have a mighty God and he provides for his children.

Then our car blew a head gasket, which meant we needed about $800. An impossibility at this time.

'I don't see how we can pay to have this done – what next?' my husband asked.

'It's okay, God will provide,' I stoutly replied. I was actually feeling excited. How was God going to fix this problem?

Then, suddenly, everyone in Australia was given an economic boost of $900. More than enough to pay the mechanic. A bit later, when things were a bit tight, we received a cheque from the tax department and it wasn't even tax time, so we were totally flummoxed by that.

These six months when Barry couldn't work were tough, but it was then that I learned about *Jehovah Jireh*[5], our Provider.

---

5   *Jehovah Jireh* is Hebrew for 'God is my provider'.

Harbouring Beauty
Catherine McAleer

I stood on a narrow brick wall that protruded from thick black muddy water and I wondered if I had any tears left. A pungent smell of salty water mixed with rotting fish filled my nostrils. Among other things, this place reeked of injustice. Was I really standing on a harbour?

Harbours conjure up images of wide expanses of tranquil, crystal blue waters, an orderly mix of boats of all shapes and sizes, and well-positioned luxury accommodation with fabulous views. This was not what lay before me as I arrived at this particular part of Manila Harbour. The water was expansive. It wasn't tranquil, nor was it crystal blue. There were boats, mostly small, questionably seaworthy fishing vessels. They weren't orderly. Accommodation was barely visible. What I could see wasn't well positioned. It was precarious at best, certainly not luxurious.

There was no turning back. We, a fellow Australian, a Filipina nun and I, had an appointment to keep. We arrived at the home of two French missionary nuns and literally stepped over the threshold. The threshold was a line of cemented-in shin-height bricks designed to keep the tide out. We sat briefly in what we later realised was a high-end dwelling in these parts. This was despite the visible evidence of large rats sharing the same space. Plans had changed. Before visiting the women of the community to share prayer, the French nuns had just learned that they needed to attend a wake. We would join them and we needed to leave now.

Fair-haired, white-skinned and standing at approximately 170cm, I drew a lot of attention, as our now party of five wove through the shipping containers, concrete-walled waterways and mud. Hands were thrust into ours and lifted to the heads of young adults, teenagers, children and babies. 'Bless! Bless!' This custom seemed strongest in communities like this. A sign of respect and honour for your elders.

During this immersion experience, I had spent much of the past two and a half months visiting economically poor communities. Life in them was unimaginably different to mine. From the outside it looked so much harder than it should have been. The disparity between the rich and the poor was shockingly evident and there seemed little hope for the future. As we navigated the pathways, I mulled over these thoughts and, I confess, only saw the negatives.

We arrived at the home of the deceased gentleman. I knew what was coming. This was my fourth wake in this part of the world but it was my fellow Australian's first. We were introduced to the family. They were indeed honoured that aside from the religious sisters, two Australians had come to visit and pay our respects to their patriarch. I greeted them but hung back as they invited us forward to view the open casket. Death is honoured differently in the Philippines to the way I was brought up and I wasn't ready to embrace this cultural difference.

Our arrival signalled the beginning of prayers. A little way off from the coffin, although close enough for me to glimpse the deceased if I looked in that direction, we gathered as a circle of believers. I hadn't been able to grasp the language during my stay but I recognised an outpouring of love, grief and unwavering faith. We mourned together. They for their husband, father, brother, uncle, community leader and friend. Me for who they had lost and, naively, for what they didn't have.

There was hardly time to wipe the tears from my eyes let alone gather the threads of my thoughts as we bade the family goodbye and threaded our way through the maze of misshapen homes towards our next stop – the women's prayer meeting. Constructed expectations of the meeting needed to be disassembled before they were fully formed. What we were about to join was not like anything I had experienced before, or since. We sat outside. There was more space and it was cooler. My position in the group allowed me to take in the concreted waist-high wall and the filthy water that lay beyond it, the gathered women, their children and a well-fed pig in its pen that seemed to be far more elaborate than the home we gathered outside of.

As the afternoon prayer began it became quite clear that the faith of these women was more than a mustard seed. They poured out their hearts, they sang, they listened and they shared. I marvelled at their ability to block out the bingo game being played at one neighbour's house and the videoke party at the other. Wannabe singers belted out eighties love songs through crackling microphones, filling any possible moments of silence. I had to concentrate hard to listen to what our translator said, often unsuccessfully. It felt like madness. Yet, these women prayed on.

Our prayer meeting was the first to break. The videoke and the bingo were just getting started. I'd been in the country and communities like this long enough to know that for some families this wouldn't end well. Family members would stagger home after a long night of singing and an over-consumption of alcohol and the stark reality of no food the following morning for others, with the day's income having been squandered away in the pursuit of Lady Luck.

Our return to the French sisters' home was not so urgent. We wandered slowly in the general direction, either deep in conversation or thought. It was decided we wouldn't walk this time. We would instead catch a ride. Our ride was a raft of sorts. Made from a packing crate and buoyed by layers of polystyrene. A woman drove us, pulling hand over hand along a rope that was strung from one concrete wall to another. As there were five of us, it was decided that my fellow Australian companion and I should go first. With some trepidation we stepped onto the small platform, each lost in our own fears and reflections of the afternoon. Our driver skilfully navigated the waterway and in no time at all she was heading back to collect the rest of our group.

Despondent and emotionally exhausted, I could see my companion was wrestling with all we had seen, heard and experienced throughout the afternoon. She looked up at me from where she sat on a low brick wall. 'Where is God in all of this?' she almost spat out. The same thought had crossed my mind. I had no answers. I looked out into the water where discarded take-away containers, plastic – so much plastic – broken rubber thongs and countless other items were being carried along by the current, hoping for an answer, something I had missed.

'There!' I almost shouted, and pointed into the floating tip. She must have thought I was mad. Amongst all the debris floated a small but beautiful, delicate lilac water lily. So out of place, yet nestled so perfectly in place.

My heart sang and my face fell. I looked and saw so many people in less-than-ideal surroundings and I failed to really see them. Beautiful people with hopes, dreams, passion and lives steeped and grounded firmly in faith. In a world where this is more than enough to go around, people still live in places that are hard to fathom and that break my heart. They don't belong in dirty harbours and yet they do. They shine because they nestle themselves perfectly into place, glorifying God's presence, living with a heart for God and blooming for all who take the time to see and admire.

The Pink Water Bottle
Charles Yuen

Haddy lived only for God ever since her conversion to the Christian faith over a decade ago. She also had a pink-coloured water bottle that she carried with her everywhere she went, which I see as a symbol of the presence of the Holy Spirit in her life. Very early in her walk with God she was at a church service when a very powerful speaker had a prophetic message to the large crowd.

'Someone in the room with a pink hat or pink top would soon find a man whom God had chosen for her,' prophesied the speaker. Haddy had been a divorced single mother for over a decade. Raising two children alone and after a painful divorce, she had virtually given up hope of finding such a man – especially not when she was in her late forties. At that age, the choices of men were usually those in their middle-ages and that meant divorced or widowed men or worse still – those who were crusty old bachelors. But nobody in that meeting wore anything matching the colour description. Hesitantly, Haddy put up her hand and asked if her pink water bottle with the pink top would qualify for the prophecy. The speaker confirmed she was indeed the recipient.

A year later, Haddy found such a man by accident. She had not been looking. Against all odds and despite much resistance from family members and friends to the suitability of the man, the couple were married only after a short period of being together. She proved them all wrong because the relationship seemed like a match made in heaven as they began serving the Lord together in love and harmony.

The Pink Water Bottle

During the couples' first Christmas together, they had a house church gathering in their home and it was a tradition for each guest to bring a small gift for exchange by lucky dip. A number was assigned by the function organiser for each gift item and a corresponding number written on a slip of paper and placed in a bowl. Being the host, Haddy was too busy in the kitchen to know about this game. But one new member, unaware of the tradition, had specifically bought two matching water bottles for the newly married couple. A blue one for her husband and a pink one for Haddy. However, the organiser insisted that the pair of bottles had to go into the lucky dip draw. While her husband knew what was going on, he somehow had a sense that the pink bottle would not go to another person and did not intervene when the organiser hijacked the pair of water bottles from the new member. Sure enough, after everyone had taken a number and were presented with their lucky gift, the last item remaining had to go to Haddy, who was still in the kitchen preparing food and too busy to even take a number slip. Sure enough, the remaining item was the pink bottle. It seems that when the Spirit has chosen you a gift, no-one can take it from you.

Later, the couple travelled to another city for business and rented a spare room in a friend's house to stay in for six weeks. They knew the room would have to be vacated for the couple's son who was planning to come home with his wife to visit them during the holiday break. Therefore, Haddy and her husband had pre-rented another place from an acquaintance for the remaining period of their stay. Unfortunately, there was a nine day gap between the two accommodations and they needed a temporary place for those days. All hotels and motels had been fully booked out in the city where they were staying because it was the peak tourist season. They had considered a road trip to some nearby towns for that period but even those remote motels were fully booked.

Then a stranger was introduced by their future landlord. The person was a widow and she had heard about the couple's housing dilemma and initially offered them the use of a spare room in her house for the nine days. It seemed like a miraculous godsend but it was one with a sting in its tail.

By this time Haddy and her husband had met another Christian couple who had invited them to worship together at their home every Saturday. Haddy was forgetful and in a habit of leaving things behind wherever she went. This time it was the pink water bottle. After attending the Saturday worship, she realised she had left the pink bottle behind. They planned to move to the widow's house the following day, so Haddy decided to collect her water bottle on the way to the new place. All their clothes had been packed into their car for the move. Even leftover food from their fridge was in an esky borrowed from the widow. It was already evening when Haddy entered the Christian couple's house to collect her water bottle. Her husband was waiting in the car when he received a call from a person claiming to be a friend and neighbour of that widow. The man was very rude and brusque. He said bluntly that the widow had made a big mistake to invite a pair of strangers to stay in her house. For all she knew the couple might take advantage of the widow's kindness. She had simply changed her mind, the invitation was withdrawn, and the spare room was no longer available. The man then hung up.

Haddy's husband was stressed. Here they were with the car full of their clothing and the food from their fridge and they were suddenly homeless. The place they had just vacated was no longer available. They could not even book into a hotel room because they knew every hotel in the city was full. Where would they be sleeping that night?

They were still parked outside the Christian couple's house and Haddy was still chatting inside with the couple's wife after collecting her pink water bottle. When the husband gave the bad news to Haddy, the Christian couple immediately offered a spare room for them in their house. In fact, they had previously been renting rooms out to other people and had two spare rooms.

During the following nine days, Haddy and her husband thoroughly enjoyed the friendship and hospitality of the Christian couple as they ate meals and worshipped daily together. This would be the beginning of a long friendship. On reflection, leaving the pink water bottle behind and collecting it at just that right moment while receiving the bad news from the fickle widow was perfectly timed. God had already arranged this perfect accommodation in advance for them.

Giving It All Up
Hannah Lamb

'I have overdosed on my medication. I am sorry. Please don't be angry.'

That's the message my mum received late one night in 2009. I was scared, I had changed my mind and I knew I needed to tell her. Her anger was clear in her voice when she called for me to come to her room. I sat in silence and shame while we drove to the hospital.

'I wish I could leave you here and go to Grandma's for a cup of tea,' Mum told me as we were waiting.

I was eventually cleared medically; however, I was too ashamed to tell the psychiatrist why I did it. I couldn't explain how I knew that I wouldn't follow through once I started taking the tablets. I didn't know how to put into words that I was in unbearable pain and distress and that I had to act, or that this was all I could think of doing, self-harm having lost its effectiveness long ago. I knew if I told them about the family dysfunction that led to this distress, they would tell Mum. I couldn't tolerate the aftermath of that. It was better for me to stay quiet.

I was left alone. The doctors were off doing paperwork, and Mum was off having a cigarette, or maybe just sitting in the waiting room away from me.

I had spent the last six months attending church, questioning and contemplating the existence of God. Curled up on the hospital bed, I decided to pray. I was done. I had nothing left in me to keep fighting, to keep living a life where there was only suffering, abandonment, and no sight of relief ahead. I was used to silence from God. I didn't expect any different in this moment, which meant that when God shared his heart with mine, it hit me twice as hard.

I love you. If you are going to give up on your life, give it up to me.

I couldn't debate that logic. I had nothing to lose by accepting God, and his request. And so, I did.

It was hospital protocol for me to see a psychiatrist. I received a call from one the next day, after school while I was with friends. He was very solemn and gentle. I confused him by answering 'Great' when he asked how I was feeling.

I went through the motions of seeing the psychiatrist, but there was little he could do for me while I was still living with my family. Many years later I would return to therapy and slowly work through everything. However, it was God who comforted me and gave me peace which got me through until I could move out. The dysfunction at home remained, but it didn't impact me as deeply. I was protected. It was his family who replaced my own, surrounding me with a love I had never known. I was given hope. I was able to live.

Colours of Childhood
Colleen Russell

I remember the colours of childhood – the people, their faces, their auras, and the flowers in our garden.

I've heard that colour is a trick of nature, an illusion, an individual perception of light, that we respond to colours through our emotions. In a happy mood, our inspiration leads us towards warm colours – vigorous reds, intense and brilliant; the joyous yellows of daisies and sunflowers; shades of orange, glowing and exuberant like the setting sun.

In a reflective mood, one can wallow in the calm serenity of blue waters, and green, too, is refreshing, the healthy abundance of nature and the environment all around us.

I remember the colours of childhood…

And I remember the white camellia tree. In autumn it blessed our family with an explosion of blossoms – a huge tree, in full bloom when we first arrived at the house. Each year my sister and I were given the job of debudding the tree to allow for more perfect blooms. These buds made great missiles in a backyard war with neighbouring children.

We had few visitors, but those that did arrive were each honoured with a photo in front of the white camellia tree, for posterity. I still have these small black and white Box Brownie prints.

Here is my sister and me standing in front of our tree, dressed in our white voile dresses, ready for Sunday School and each bearing a lovely white camellia for the teacher.

I remember the colours of scents and senses...

My mother was a member of the Rose Society, and dozens of rose bushes flourished against the paling fence in our yard. She tended each one with loving care, entered her blooms in Rose Society exhibitions, and proudly brought home her awards.

Each morning we set off with a fresh rose pinned to our lapels, bearing all day the heady perfume of American Beauty, scarlet; the Duke of Edinburgh, a rich red; the lovely Peace climber of palest pink; and my favourite Charles Mallerin, highly fragrant, a double hybrid tea rose, dark red like the blood that dripped from my finger tip pierced by its thorns.

On the first day of September we celebrated Wattle Day. In the gully below our house the yellow acacias bloomed, early harbingers of spring, our national floral emblem. We garnered armsful for vases, together with furry creamy catkins of pussy willow. It was said that it was bad luck to have wattle in the house, I think because it caused allergies for some, but our house was blessed.

The back lawn of Grandfather's small house had been taken over by heartsease, miniature pansies, their little faces of yellow and purple smiling openly at the sun. We laughed when Grandfather told us some of the whimsical names that people gave these tiny flowers –

tickle-me-fancy, Jack-jump-up-and-kiss-me, come-and-cuddle-me. Grandma brought their cheer inside, massed in a shallow bowl on the table. And they gave Grandfather an excuse for not mowing the lawn.

On Sunday mornings I was overwhelmed by a kaleidoscope of colours – shimmering reds, greens, blues, yellows, slipping and sliding in the sunbeams that flickered through the stained glass windows of our old stone church. Memories of the lessons escape me, because I was too busy watching the dust motes bouncing in the multi-coloured lights, the fairy dancers of my childhood, performing to music from the organ, as the congregation raised their voices in exaltation to praise our Lord.

And I remember our pets, colourful characters in a different sense of the word.

At one time we had a pink and grey galah, boss cocky of the house, who chased our black kelpie and the cats, nipping at their feet with its sharp beak.

Our cats – the ginger female, unusual, as most ginger cats are male; the other dumpy and placid, pure white with silver tips when caught in the right light. She allowed me to dress her in doll's clothes, wrap her in a blanket and place her in a doll's cradle, where she would stay for hours, forgotten and contented, until mealtime.

And I remember the people – my carrot-haired cousin with her fair skin, a procession of freckles skipping gaily across her cheeks.

Now as she ages, her hair is hoary white, like a mountain snowcap shining in the sun. The freckles are still there, but faded, as she is fading.

When I look at my daughter, I see her bright blue intelligent eyes, my grandmother's eyes, which were always hidden behind gold-rimmed glasses, alert to notice any childish misdemeanours.

Nana was small and agile, impetuous, full of life, forever prepared with a weird story, about weird people. I remember her telling us of a lady of her acquaintance, who had a long tapeworm inside, which popped its head out of her mouth as she spoke! Another friend collected garden snails for dinner, fried in garlic butter. Delicious!

On Nana's 80th birthday we gave her a bunch of artificial violets to wear on her lapel, highly fashionable then. She graciously declined them. 'Thank you, my dears, but violets are only for old ladies. But they do remind me of a lady I once knew, who wore violets hanging from her eyebrows, long before pierced eyebrows became fashionable with the young…!'

Once on my mother's birthday, we presented her with a dozen daffodils and I still remember the glow the flowers gave to her face. My sister and I sang:

You are my sunshine, my only sunshine,

You make me happy when skies are grey

and her face glowed more from the pleasure of it all.

Now when I look at my son, I see my mother's thick dark hair, glossy strands of wellbeing. I'm tempted to stroke his head, so lustrous and alive, like the fur of some friendly beast.

And when I look in the mirror, I see my father's hazel eyes laughing back at me.

All these loved ones, some long gone, but still here with me, living on in the course of colourful memories, down through the generations.

I remember the colours and the senses and the people surrounded by God's love.

And I remember the colours of childhood…

Along for the Ride
Ruth C Hall

You know that feeling when you're on holiday and you see something amazing which makes you turn to your companion to express your feelings of awe; how having someone there with you brings more to the experience?

Well, several years ago I was on a three-month solo driving and camping trip. Exploring spectacular countryside, I would come across the crest of a hill and see some huge lake, or an animal crossing the road, and I'd have loved to share the actual moment with someone. I posted pictures online and sent them to friends and family. But that wasn't the same and, in a way, being alone diminished the enjoyment. In fact, sometimes I felt quite lonely amongst the beauty.

Now, Jesus was and still is someone I talk to often during the day. He's supported me in very dark times and I've often chatted with him in my mind. So, knowing God was with me, I started pretending that Jesus was sitting right next to me in the car, and began chatting out loud to him, as I would to a human person. Exclamations like, 'Wow, Jesus – look at that,' became commonplace.

I wasn't officially 'praying,' I wasn't asking anything or offloading my problems to him. I was just enjoying the scene with a friend. He was there and enjoying it with me, like another person would. A new aspect to our relationship developed as he became a tangible friend.

Being someone who loves a good joke and seeing the funny side in everyday life, I found I was often laughing with him too.

One evening I was free-camping in an area which had quite a few campers. I'd found what looked a quiet spot next to a track which led to the beach. Around 10pm, I was about to settle for the night in my tent, so I headed outside to relieve myself in the bushes. It was a peaceful evening and, thinking everyone was settling too, I just went to the edge of the vegetation. It was as I'd finished but still in a squatting position that I suddenly heard voices, and a torch came into view – there were people walking down the track!

The fright of them suddenly appearing startled me and, still crouched, I spun around. Thankfully I was well-hidden behind my car. But that movement caused me to slip and fall back onto the ground – the wet ground. So there I was, sitting in the sodden dirt, trying to be very quiet while stifling my laughter, knowing this would be a great story to tell my friends.

And then, as I waited in my puddle for the walkers to pass by, I found myself giggling with my friend Jesus about it. I'm sure he thought it was hilarious too. I loved that I was able to include him in something so rudimentary. And I think he loved that I was allowing him to become closer to me in a human way.

Out of the Ashes
Barbara McKay

It was Good Friday at 'Sunshine Cottage'. The morning sky was ablaze with fiery colours. A brilliant palette of amazing reds and oranges flooded the celestial sphere. Little did I know that this day would end with these same shades in a dramatic turn of events. Sober thoughts from my swirling mind drew me to attention. 'Donald and I should be attending worship together.'

Easter had always been the busiest time of the year. Whilst I felt slightly envious of those who went camping, on the flip side, being married to a preacher was a privilege. It wasn't a four-day holiday, but the proclamation of an amazing story with pastoral care for all who satisfied their conscience with 'once-a year' attendance. Over forty years, preparation for the Passover meal, Good Friday and Easter Sunday had been our total focus.

After being hospitalised in Toowoomba with neutropenia, Donald was home and immunosuppressed. With cells continuing to metastasise from prostate cancer, I could see his walking was slow, and the furrows on his brow revealed the severity of his pain. I said to him as I prepared breakfast, 'Donald, let's have a quiet day. You need to be isolated. We're *not* going to church. Let's have our own Good Friday service.'

We read afresh the gospel accounts of Good Friday and recalled our family trip to Golgotha in 1990. As we meditated again on the sufferings of Christ, we thanked God for the gift of his Son.

A peace descended upon us. Not for one moment, did we contemplate that later that day we would experience our own crucifying experience.

That evening, Donald rolled up a piece of newspaper. 'Barbara, we need to burn that wasp nest.' We walked 100 metres to our shed, the size of a small aircraft hangar. Wasps had built a large nest high under the awning, and because we couldn't reach the spot, we lit the newspaper.

Within seconds, a wisp of wind transported the flame to the polystyrene boxes which the previous owner had placed on the roof of the cold room for extra insulation. Billows of black smoke filled the night sky as foam began to burn and spread.

Smoke choked my lungs as I yelled, 'Donald, triple 0. Have you rung?'

His urgent plea escalated to utter desperation. 'I can't get through. No reception.'

The more he tried, the harder it became. Darkness closed in.

With complete knowledge of his chemotherapy brain fog, and the fact that he was high on morphine, I shouted. 'Give me your phone. I'll do it.'

'No, I'll go to the top of the hill – see if I can get reception there.'

Disappointment set in as we realised our predicament, and as each second ticked over, my voice crackled, 'Why hasn't the fire brigade arrived?'

Donald gasped as he spoke. 'Quick, Barb, we need to get the vehicles out. You drive your car and I'll drive the BT 50.' With flames devouring everything in their path, we rushed into the shed. The heat had intensified, and as we saw the tongues of flames spreading and felt the scorching on our bodies, we jumped into the cars and drove them out – then rushed back again to drive out two tractors.

The fire engulfed our precious belongings. With all the drums of fuel, gas bottles and oil, we knew the flames would soon turn into an explosive inferno. My head was spinning. I was exhausted to the point of physical collapse. I raced over to our house to grab my iPad. 'I'll film this.' With a thumping headache, I didn't realise I was breathing in toxic, carcinogenic particles.

I raced back to the fire as black, surging smoke and fire consumed every panel in the cold room. It was as if someone had thrown a bomb, with debris flying in all directions. I stood back, and kept filming. The destructive fireworks intensified. Ammunition from Donald's gun safe, paint and fuel tins exploded. I didn't see Donald rush around to the back of the shed to the fresh water tank but I heard his loud, panicky voice yelling 'Barbara, stay away from the fire. You'll be killed.'

'Where is the fire brigade? Why aren't they here?' I yelled several times with every word becoming more and more urgent, as if fighting for survival. Smoke and flames continued to choke and dry my throat, and with every breath, I kept spitting as I breathed in black particles.

Eventually, the fire brigade arrived. They set up their high-pressure water hose, aiming it at the shed. Remaining calm, one firie tried to reassure me. Repeatedly, I shouted, 'Go into the shed...my husband's library...a thousand books...you must save them.'

I don't have any recollection of the continuing saga, but I remember sitting on the grass outside the back door of our house in a daze. The ambo crouched next to me. 'Come over to the ambulance. We'll check you out.'

Gasping for breath and crying, I answered in an adamant, disorientated tone, 'No, I'm a nurse and I'm not injured. You have to put the fire out.' Obviously, I was in extreme shock, and with the iPad in my hand, I had walked outside and fainted. Consciousness returned. I kept repeating, 'I've hit my head. I've hit my head.'

I touched my forehead, and felt a rough spot. That small abrasion reminded me that I *had* experienced a fall.

Taking me by the hand, he helped me up. 'Come with me to the ambulance. We will take you and your husband to the Gatton Hospital to be checked out.'

Sitting in the ambulance, I looked across at Donald with his burnt, bandaged hand. How extensive were his injuries? I wondered.

Years later, I read the ambulance report.

BP 165/96 'Confusion' noted at 1945hrs. Patient has soot on her face and bottom lip, but no singeing to eyebrows or nasal area. Patient denies any shortness of breath or difficulty with breathing.

She denies any headache or chest pain. Patient developed emotional repetitive amnesia and had difficulty recalling the event. She refused oxygen and intravenous access.

After one night of neurological observations, I was transferred to an Ipswich hospital. I lay in bed disoriented and dazed, the cogs in my brain barely turning. Hospitalisation meant forced rest and the opportunity to recuperate. Whilst I didn't understand the full impact of stress and shock, the amnesia was a protective mechanism in my brain, like a trip switch. It shuts down if overloaded in order to protect. Hospitalisation meant I had crashed hard and had nothing left in my emotional tank.

Over four years, I had coped with the anxiety of Donald's clinical emergencies. Now a double whammy. How would I find strength to care for my dear Donald in his final months? Where would I find courage to face the aftermath of such a disastrous fire? It had destroyed his entire theological library of over 1000 books, including an office built by a nephew. Irreplaceable, personal possessions stored by our adult children were also burnt.

In hospital, I had time to rest, reflect and steady my mind. Prior to discharge after ten days, I asked for a day pass. I went for a walk. I discovered the Incinerator Theatre. In the early 1960's, the Ipswich Little Theatre asked the council not to demolish this significant building, but to restore it and make it into a theatre. I saw a plaque in a well-designed garden. On a mosaic sculpture were the words 'Rising from the Ashes' – a practical example of beauty in the midst of destruction.

I savoured this moment. It was as if a thousand bouquets of joy had been dropped at my feet. Glistening tears rolled down my cheeks and I welcomed the euphoria. Just as a tender voice spoke to Mary Magdalene long ago on that first Easter morning, it seemed that his love reached out with heavenly hugs. In a warm, affectionate voice, he seemed to say, 'Look at me, Barb. You, too, will rise from the ashes.'

Donald's injuries in the fire were not serious. He returned from hospital, and needed care from loved ones. When he died five months later, I read his journal. Knowing his great difficulty in sharing emotions, his words speak volumes. Donald often struggled to express his love for me verbally, but his hand-written words after that horrendous Good Friday fire, give comfort and hope.

We have had a disaster like no other….the shed burnt down, destroying a lifetime of memories. Barbara and I are still alive. I am reading Psalm 91 (all my commentaries are burnt). I have been 'melting down'. I don't normally cry. It's hard to see what good thing can come from this accident, but Romans 8:28 says 'In all things God works for the good of those who love Him.'

Dear Friend
Jo-Anne Berthelsen

It is some months since I last visited my friend in the nursing home. As I make my way to her room, I hope and pray she will still recognise me. At the door, I see a nurse settling her into her special, comfortable wheelchair. Then my friend turns towards me and her face lights up.

'Oh! What a…what a…sur…oh!'

I grasp her hand as she gazes at me in wonderment.

'I'll take her to the sunroom – you can chat more easily there,' the nurse tells us with a smile.

For some time, my friend continues to search my face with loving eyes. I suspect my name has slipped her mind but I resist the urge to tell her. It does not matter anyway – I am sure she realises who I am. I remind her of our book *Soul Friend* that I wrote about our journey together during my years at theological college, then on into ministry and writing.

'Yes, *Soul Friend*,' she says softly after a few moments – and I know then that she remembers.

I talk with her about her family and mine. I share some special biscuits I often used to bake for her and she remembers those too. It is hard for her to hold them now and they tend to break easily. The crumbs they leave behind on her clothes seem to disturb her, so I try to help her brush them off. We look at each other then and laugh – a laugh that is beautiful music to my ears because it reminds me vividly of other shared moments of joy.

She has not changed. She is still the same precious person deep inside. She may have trouble completing sentences. She may grope for the words she wants to say. She may not remember names so easily. Yet she is still my dear soul friend out of whose face the love of God continues to shine.

Eventually, I notice she is beginning to tire. A nurse comes to wheel her to another area and I prepare to say goodbye. I hold her hand and give her a kiss.

'Oh, thank you, thank you, thank you! There's nothing like a kiss,' she says, closing her eyes in ecstasy.

'Then I'll give you another one,' I tell her, dropping a second light kiss on her forehead.

Now her face is suffused with pure joy. When I hold her hand one last time before leaving, I hear those beautiful, familiar words that have always felt like a blessing from her to me – 'Dear friend.'

I drive away, sadness welling up inside me. Then I hear another gentle voice, speaking into my spirit.

'Dear friend,' it says too.

I know this is the voice of my heavenly Father, reaching out to me, his child – his friend. Human minds may falter. Earthly friends may fade and disappear. Yet nothing can ever separate me from my Father's love – and I am deeply comforted.

Guitar Strums
Diana Davison

My eyes opened before the alarm rang out, at 6.30 am. I jumped out of bed and got myself ready to head to the airport. It was a straightforward journey with no delays predicted. Setbacks would only add unnecessary frustration or an unwanted sprint in shoes not crafted for running, in between transit stops and catching the next flight. I made this all-day long haul trip more comfortable with forced movie bingeing without guilt.

On final touchdown, the tame Friday evening atmosphere presented a welcoming relief. The arrival terminal appeared idle, like the lengthy and lazy line of taxis waiting. I had swapped one tropical climate – Queensland – for another – Sarawak, Borneo. It was the start of autumn in Australia with no signs of cooling down. This overseas environment sat dipped in the rainy season, with predictable daily showers that encouraged the day to bring cool to clammy.

I arrived at the hotel just before midnight. Steven stood behind the counter, waiting to greet late arrivals – me. I paid the deposit, took the swipe key and made my way to the lift to head up to the fourth floor. The lodgings were simple, clean, and all I needed. Perfect for my fortnight stay. Each mission to this semi-sleepy town is to visit and support my mother during the waning of her life. These solo trips also acted to rekindle the bond of mother and daughter. My 85-year-old mother, diagnosed with a spreading stage IV cancer, required extra doses of patience and understanding. We both did. This was not a holiday for sight-seeing excursions. Any 'me time' came at the end of day in the privacy and solitude of my room.

I knew this trip would not differ from the last – a rough roller coaster with more downs than ups. The sensitive sorting of a lifetime of my mother's personal hoarding was upsetting and depressing. Belongings that told her story. An overload of furniture, clothes, ornaments, kitchenware. The layers of hundreds of photographs taken over decades now posed sadly in boxes and more boxes. Plus two enormous tin trunks. All of which needed to be looked at, divided between siblings, relatives and disposed of accordingly. My mother had thought she could cope after my father's passing just before Covid. But the pandemic made sure she stayed lonely and isolated. For me, the trips have definitely been a tearful and painstaking toil – a continual reminder of his absence.

It didn't take long, just forty-eight hours, for the days to all blend into one lengthy repetition. Sunday was nearly over. I returned to my hotel room, a peaceful refuge. It had been another hard spell at my mother's house, run-down and way out in the sticks. The whole situation, like Groundhog Day, was never ending. After a laborious day sorting, it was time for a visit to my mother at the care home facility – a reluctant new resident. By now, I'd mastered the art of conversation that swerved and skirted away from anything to do with her stuff. That would only cause upset and unwanted questions to deal with. A definite drain, being constantly cautious.

Guitar Strums

When daylight thinned out, it was time for the cold beer in the fridge begging to be popped open and supped. My weary and worried mind needed relaxation therapy. Upon entering the room, I flicked on the air-conditioning, grabbed an icy Tiger beer and settled down with my private thoughts to the hissing sound of the opening beer can. A sigh of relief sounded from both drink and drinker. It already seemed like I'd been there a week, but it was only my second day. Arranging transport to each port of call and driving in-between rain falls, keeping my feelings in check until I made it back to the hotel became a daily juggle. Internal conversations and reflections came alive when alone in the confines of my cosy space. I looked forward to my company and required timeout in the silence of my quarters.

Within ten minutes of sitting, surprise caught me. Sailing through the walls from the next room – 408 – emanated the melancholy strumming of a guitar. Uncertain if my mind was playing tricks, I stopped what little I was doing and remained still. It continued, the same slow, sombre tune. Could I be the sole audience?

I listened to the stranger play. A weird sense to be alone and yet suddenly have somebody comfortingly close by that I couldn't see. An unknown figure caressing the instrument in a world of their own, while I lingered listening. Both in this calm, colourful city tucked away in Borneo. Someone mindfully stringing together each note to feed my curiosity and fuel my creativity. The night abruptly took on an engaging and unforeseen turn – a lulling mystery. The smooth strumming sound immediately soothed me. An unfamiliar tune with no hurry to its slow melody. Almost like a snake charmer, without the snake or basket – just charming. There was a foreignness about its methodical rhythm. My trip had only begun. Maybe this random person in room 408 was at the end of their trip. I didn't know, but appreciated the companionship with no strings attached. Definitely better than the television programs that hovered between clear and static pictures and the heavy thought-load of my mother.

As the days passed, the sound of these mystical melodies became part of the tranquil room ritual. As soon as I detected the first note, I would immediately stop in my tracks, as if in a game of statues. A moment to centre, listen and then carry on with whatever I was doing. I conjured up scenes to go along with the guitar soundtracks. An entertaining pastime with every tune. Each embraced, performance uncertain and unannounced – morning, afternoon, and night. Despite having commitments outside of my temporary bedroom, the music sessions were enough to make me have to fight the urge to stay in and wait for the next strumming. My interest grew steadily. I wondered about the secret stranger – what the individual looked like. Had I already seen this person, perhaps at breakfast, without knowing it?

The riddle continued every time the door to room 408 opened. Quick as a blink, I'd dash to the peephole of my door, 409. But the hallway rolled out too far right to get a clear view. After three days of the same music, I was keen now to steal a glimpse of this guest. The hypnotic hook was haunting. I sometimes worried when the silence dragged on for too long. Had they left? I tracked the comings and goings by the sound of the next door opening and closing and the chiming ping of the lift a few seconds later.

The subsequent days presented busy as usual, and evenings brought a pleasant treat. After returning to my room one day, the gentle strumming echoed out about 8.30pm. But this time, a mellow vocal to accompany the guitar emerged. One veil of intrigue picked away. A male voice. It softly sailed on a melody through the separating barrier. I couldn't help a smile as I headed to the corner of the room where the sound travelled the strongest. And, like a magnet, I pinned my ear to the wall. It felt naughty being intrusive, but I was inquisitive. I listened hard. It wasn't easy to make out the foreign lyrics. The partition made the ballad unclear and my neck started hurting from being pressed to one side too long, straining for a clue. It didn't stop my muse from plucking impressions out of thin air. The melancholy expression and the low strum transmitted as if on a loop.

The trip panned out better than expected. Ten days had now gone by and the late afternoon saw me comfortably sitting in my room enjoying some background strumming from the mystery melody man. I was unusually relaxed. Daily, someone had conducted me away from the stresses and strains.

After two weeks of being there for my mother, it ended all too quickly. There were some trying moments. It was necessary to be 'up' all the time for her so that she would gain strength to stay positive. Leaving her behind until my return was always unsettling. But with this journey, I knew I was not alone. I never met the anonymous acoustic angel. I didn't need to. Each serenade that greeted me in the mornings when I woke and in the evenings before I slept presented as a gift. The invisible neighbour sent to comfort and calm me, allowing clarity. The unavoidable, arduous load lightened. Those guitar strums were a blessing in disguise. A grounding and guiding presence watched over me. One I could not see but wholeheartedly heard.

People Matter
Kylie Gardiner

I first noticed him as he stood and watched us run the lunchtime program every Friday at our local secondary school. He would look on as fifty or more students ran around participating in all kinds of fun activities but he would shake his head when asked to join in. He preferred to watch from his hideout under the roof of the footy shed, eating a sandwich.

He was a slight boy with shaggy blond hair that fell over his face. Slowly, slowly, week by week the ice broke. We discovered he had recently emigrated from Finland and his name was Matias. He didn't know much English, only swear words as they were the most common words thrown at him. The first breakthrough was when he came over and stood with a leader.

Next, I asked him to hold things. He held the net for water balloon volleyball. The stick for the limbo. The target for the footy handball competition. He began to laugh as he watched the chaos. He morphed into a junior leader. He'd have the lollies ready for prizes. He'd draw the lucky door. He helped us pack up after the first bell had gone, when we knew that would make him late for class, but he was determined to pitch in.

He stepped up and told everyone our norms at the start of the program – build people up, help people grow, because people matter. But there were still students that would tell him to disappear. Tell him he was a loser with no friends. Tell him to go back to where he came from. He'd cop an 'accidental' shove as he collected equipment. His clothes didn't have the worn in look of most of the students. His were crisp and smart. He was the only student we ever saw with a tie.

One day I dropped into the school office. There was Matias sitting on a chair outside the principal's office. The receptionist saw me look at him.

'He's there every recess and lunchtime, poor thing. He's not in trouble, it's just the only place he feels safe.'

'Except for Friday lunch,' the other office lady called out. 'When you guys are here.'

Then it happened. The wheelbarrow races. A group of Year Ten boys made a team. They were deciding who was to sit in the wheelbarrow. They looked each other over to see who was the smallest and lightest. Then they looked at this quiet Finnish boy. They sized him up.

'What's ya name?'

'Matias,' he replied.

'Well, come on, Matty, jump in the barrow.' And so he did and he couldn't stop laughing as he bounced around. He became part of the group. He gained some respect. He made a few friendships. We introduced him to students we felt would look out for him. Gradually there were fewer recess and lunch times spent sitting outside the principal's office. Matias means gift of God and he was our gift – to show us the way to include.

Terracotta Travellers
Grant Lock

It all happened yesterday. The bus was fairly full. Then came the noise. Loud then louder. It was hip-hop…and very LOUD.

I think it is coming from the seat in front of me, where the teenage girl is holding up her phone. No, it's from the seat just behind me. I half turn, and it's a big guy in a black hoodie. Well, no one else seemed to be concerned about this huge audio invasion of our personal space. I hold my position for a bit, just to get the message across: there is at least one person who thinks otherwise.

The volume drops a bit. I turn back, and exhale. Mission accomplished. Now I can at least hear my audio book through my headset.

But Mr Hoodie is not happy. The noise level comes up, and up and up. Much more than before. And now there are regular F words in the staccato rhymes. Everyone else stares straight ahead, like a busload of pairs of terracotta warriors, pretending that nothing is happening. And now the F-words are multiplying in the loudness. But they all hold that terracotta stare, the men, the women, the girls, the boys.

It looks like I'll have to try again. I turn hard in my seat and glare directly at Mr Hip-hop Hoodie. I hold my gaze. And despite my lack of central vision, I note the guy is much bigger than I thought.

And he is no longer wearing a black hoodie. It's a black balaclava. Just like they use to rob banks and petrol stations, and terrorists use in Syria.

What's this guy doing on the bus? And what's in that backpack beside him?

The balaclava leans forward, and speaks. It's a strong voice with a slow dash of venom. 'Can I help you?'

Well, I'm not giving up that easily, but I'd better be circumspect in my response.

'Yes,' I reply, 'I have a big problem with blindness,' and I have to half-shout, 'but I don't have any problem with my hearing!'

By now every terracotta eye has amazingly turned our way.

He leans forward a bit more, and shouts back, 'I want *everyone* to hear the lyrics,' and he scans around. '*Everyone!*'

I don't like his tone, and I'm not used to being in such close quarters with aggressive black balaclavas. So I'd better not be too direct in making suggestions about his precious music.

'Well,' I shout, 'I know a bit about lyrics. I'm a writer.'

The hip-hop noise level immediately drops. 'So…what do you write?'

'I've written a couple of books. The first one is called *Shoot Me First.*' Somehow, I find one of my book cards to thrust into his hand.

Black Balaclava stares at the card, then scans me in my Afghan Pakhol hat, the same hat I'm wearing in my picture on the book card.

'Unreal! Unreal! *You*…are the bloke who wrote this book?'

I nod. I'm not sure what is coming next.

'Unreal,' he gushes on. 'I've got this book. I got it yesterday in the Salvos bookshop. I was checking books on the shelves and this one dropped out. I picked it up and said, "Righto, this is the one I'm taking." Unreal.'

The bus pulls up at the Parliament House bus stop. I get up.

He rises. 'I'm getting our here too. Meeting a mate.'

We get out and the Balaclava is eyeballing me. 'I can't believe it!' he says. He pumps my hand. 'I'm so pleased to meet you. I can't believe it. What a coincidence! Unreal.'

I return the shake and grip his hand. 'What's your name?'

'Shane,' he says.

'Well, Shane, I'm pleased to meet you too. And,' I add, 'it's not a coincidence at all. It's a God thing. Just like it was a God thing that took us to Afghanistan and Pakistan.'

It's hard for anyone to read the expression behind a black balaclava, but his whole tone has changed.

'I've got to tell my mates,' he says. 'And I'm going to start reading your book. Tonight!'

'Shane,' I say, 'I have to catch a train out to Salisbury, but if you ever want to catch up, my email address is on the bottom of that book card. It would be great to hear from you.'

'Yeah. Yeah,' he says, 'that would be really great,' and he pumps my hand again.

As my white stick and I tap tap past Parliament House to the train station, I can still hear his, 'Unreals' in the distance.

Well, I don't know what happened to those terracotta travellers, but the black balaclava is no longer a black balaclava…he is Shane. And I hope he makes contact again.

It's over to you, Lord.

Isn't it time you told your story?

This year, 37 people have had their stories published, and seven of them have been recognised as category winners. Do you have a story of faith and testimony? Will 2024 be the year you tell your story?

For the possibility of being published or winning a prize, please send us your true stories in one of these categories:

Open Category
maximum 1500 words

Short Category
maximum 500 words

Submission details, rules and writing resources can be found on our website:

https://storiesoflife.net

Have you written a book?
Not sure how to get it published?
Worried it will cost a fortune?

Not a problem.

Helping writers to become authors

info@immortalise.com.au
www.immortalise.com.au

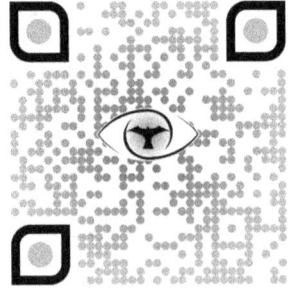

www.ingramcontent.com/pod-product-compliance
Lightning Source LLC
Chambersburg PA
CBHW070255010526
44107CB00056B/2468